D0914399

how to
know the
aquatic
plants

The **Pictured Key Nature Series** has been published since 1944 by the Wm. C. Brown Company. The series was initiated in 1937 by the late Dr. H. E. Jaques, Professor Emeritus of Biology at Iowa Wesleyan University. Dr. Jaques' dedication to the interest of nature lovers in every walk of life has resulted in the prominent place this series fills for all who wonder **"How to Know."**

John F. Bamrick and Edward T. Cawley
Consulting Editors

The Pictured Key Nature Series

How to Know the
AQUATIC INSECTS, Lehmkuhl
AQUATIC PLANTS, Prescott
BEETLES, Arnett-Downie-Jaques, Second Edition
BUTTERFLIES, Ehrlich
ECONOMIC PLANTS, Jaques, Second Edition
FALL FLOWERS, Cuthbert
FERNS AND FERN ALLIES, Mickel
FRESHWATER ALGAE, Prescott, Third Edition
FRESHWATER FISHES, Eddy-Underhill, Third Edition
GILLED MUSHROOMS, Smith-Smith-Weber
GRASSES, Pohl, Third Edition
IMMATURE INSECTS, Chu
INSECTS, Bland-Jaques, Third Edition
LAND BIRDS, Jaques
LICHENS, Hale, Second Edition
LIVING THINGS, Jaques, Second Edition
MAMMALS, Booth, Third Edition
MARINE ISOPOD CRUSTACEANS, Schultz
MITES AND TICKS, McDaniel
MOSSES AND LIVERWORTS, Conard-Redfearn, Third Edition
NON-GILLED FLESHY FUNGI, Smith-Smith
PLANT FAMILIES, Jaques
POLLEN AND SPORES, Kapp
PROTOZOA, Jahn, Bovee, Jahn, Third Edition
SEAWEEDS, Abbott-Dawson, Second Edition
SEED PLANTS, Cronquist

SPIDERS, Kaston, Third Edition
SPRING FLOWERS, Cuthbert, Second Edition
TREMATODES, Schell
TREES, Miller-Jaques, Third Edition
TRUE BUGS, Slater-Baranowski
WATER BIRDS, Jaques-Ollivier
WEEDS, Wilkinson-Jaques, Third Edition
WESTERN TREES, Baerg, Second Edition

how to know the

aquatic plants

Second Edition

G. W. Prescott
University of Montana
Biological Station

The Pictured Key Nature Series
Wm. C. Brown Company Publishers
Dubuque, Iowa

THE HOLDEN ARBORETUM
LIBRARY

Copyright © 1969, 1980 by Wm. C. Brown Company Publishers

Library of Congress Catalog Card Number: 78-72987

ISBN 0-697-04775-X (Paper)

ISBN 0-697-04774-1 (Cloth)

All rights reserved. No part of this publication may be reproduced,
stored in a retrieval system, or transmitted, in any form or by any
means, electronic, mechanical, photocopying, recording, or otherwise,
without the prior written permission of the copyright owner.

Printed in the United States of America

5193
THE HOLDEN ARBORETUM.
LIBRARY.

Contents

Preface

More and more attention is being directed toward aquatic biota with the ever-mounting interest in water quality and quantity. The importance of the roles that algae and higher plants play in the water realm cannot be over-emphasized, and it is because of various interests in aquatic vegetation that this synopsis was prepared. The following key to aquatic plant genera was written for those who may not be experienced botanists, but who wish an introduction to plants in the aquatic environment, and to know their names.

The genera included in this edition are the most common or more frequently seen in the United States, although in some sections of the country (coastal swamps, the arid southwest and the lower Mississippi valley) there are some genera locally common which are not treated. Because of the length of the key in the former edition, it has been deemed inadvisable to extend it to include more genera. A list of references to less abridged works is given for those who wish additional information.

Each genus is illustrated and for some, more than one species is depicted to help give an idea of the variations within a genus. The illustrations were prepared from living specimens whenever possible. Others have been drawn (and sometimes stylized) from her-barium specimens. In this new edition some additional illustrations are included, as for *Potamogeton*, *e.g.*, a genus which includes many and varied species. Also drawings have been added to differentiate *Elodea* and *Hydrilla*, the latter being a plant very similar to *Elodea* and possibly confused with it. Also some illustrations have been modified to more correctly illustrate species and to remove inconsistencies.

The distribution range of genera in the United States has been extended following more recent publications on aquatic plants, and a discussion of their ecology has been introduced. This section includes a list of the common plants in reference to zonation and water depth. Also in this new edition is a brief description of the more obvious morphological characters of aquatic plants which are related to ecological factors and which are seen to be adaptations.

Whenever appropriate, the economic and/or biological importances of respective genera are pointed out in descriptive notes within the key. The family relationship of each genus is included in the legends of illustrations and a check list of aquatic plant genera within their respective families is appended. The illustrated glossary-index should assist in understanding descriptive terms used in the text.

The new format used for this edition, with an increase in size of illustrations, results in a more readable work which it is hoped will be appreciated.

The author is grateful to Dr. W. C. Vinyard and Dr. John H. Thomas for their help and wishes to acknowledge with thanks the facilities provided by the Department of Botany and the Biological Station of the University of Montana.

Introduction

In the United States there are about 1,300 species of aquatic or semi-aquatic plants in some 306 genera, and representing about 65 families. These numbers include many species which may be only incidentally present in moist or marshy situations and are subject to the definitive limitations drawn by respective botanists who have written about them. Some 165 of these genera are included in the synoptic key to follow wherein an attempt has been made to include mostly the truly aquatic plants and also those which are characteristically and commonly present in bogs, marshes and along shore lines.

When all the aquatic plant species are placed in review it is noteworthy that a majority are in the Monocotyledonae of the seed plants, although more of the genera are in the Dicotyledonae (primarily because there are more dicot genera in nature than monocot.). Further, it is noted that of the families which are entirely aquatic in the United States, 9 are Monocotyledonae and only 3 (possibly 4) belong to the Dicotyledonae.

The Divisions (Phyla) and subgroups (Classes) which comprise the plant kingdom are listed for reference. Those groups which are considered in this work are indicated by (*).

    I. Chlorophyta (Green Algae)*
   II. Euglenophyta (Euglenoid Algae)
  III. Chrysophyta (Yellow-green Algae)
  IV. Cryptophyta (Chrysophyte Algae)
   V. Pyrrhophyta (Dinoflagellate Algae)
  VI. Cyanophyta (Blue-green Algae)
 VII. Phaeophyta (Brown Algae: Seaweeds)
VIII. Rhodophyta (Red Algae: Seaweeds)*
  IX. Chloromonadophyta (Chloromonad Algae)
   X. Bryophyta
      A. Hepaticae (Liverworts)*
      B. Musci (Mosses)*
  XI. Psilopsida (Psilophyte Ferns)
 XII. Lycopsida (Club Moss Pteridophytes)
XIII. Sphenopsida (Horse Tail Ferns)*
XIV. Pteropsida (Ferns)*
 XV. Spermatophyta (Seed Plants)
      A. Gymnospermae*
      B. Angiospermae*
          1. Monocotyledonae*
          2. Dicotyledonae*

Importances and Uses
of Aquatic Plants

Aquatic plants have both positive and negative importances to Man, either directly or indirectly. Anyone who fishes, swims or boats in lakes and lagoons is well-aware that water vegetation is often obnoxiously abundant. One sometimes wonders what the plants are and what might be done to eradicate them.

Aquatic animals, as well as some terrestrial or semi-terrestrial ones such as moose and muskrat, use water plants for food. Both aquatic and upland birds obtain much of their food from aquatic plants directly, or indirectly from the small animals in the water which depend on aquatic plants and algae. Fish use aquatic plants directly or they too feed upon the small animals that live on and around them. Some kinds of fish (sunfish, perch) have their nests in beds of aquatic plants. Many aquatic insects live on and in plants, spending all or part of their life history here, using them for food, for egg-laying or for emergence.

Not a few species of aquatic plants are directly important to Man for food and for materials. Indian Rice, Water Chestnut and Delta Potato are sources of food. In some parts of the world the Bulrush is used for the building of boats, for floor mats and wall partitions.

Limnologically aquatic plants and shoreline vegetation play important roles such as beach-building, the filling in of lake margins with the accompanying aging and eutrophication, and prevention of shore erosion. A few aquatic plants bring about the deposition of lime, thus, after a long period of time, produce useful marl deposits. In addition to these relationships it must be recalled that there are many interactions between aquatic plants and water chemistry and the nature of bottom deposits.

Further, students of plant morphology, physiology and plant evolution find aquatic plants of rewarding interest. Most plants in the water have about the same relationship to terrestrial relatives that aquatic mammals such as whales and dolphins have to land animals. The aquatic plants, to a large extent, are representatives of evolutionary developments which, after having developed to an advanced state on land, have become adjusted to and have 'returned' to an aquatic environment. The morphological and physiological changes required to meet the problems of an aquatic existence invite scientific studies and considerable speculation.

Ecological Relationships

Aquatic plant species, like most aquatic organisms, are more widely distributed throughout the world than terrestrial. This is so mostly because factors or conditions required by aquatic plants are more uniform in general than are those to which land plants must make adjustment. Water temperature, water chemistry and life-giving nutrients are less variable. Yet species are selective of their habitat, so much so that a combination of species often can be used as an index of physical-chemical conditions within a body of water. Whereas most species, perhaps, thrive well in and often require organic bottom sediments, others are adapted to and are found only in sandy-bottom habitats. Many are capable of growing in deep water where light is subdued, and do not need to reach the surface (some spp. of *Potamogeton, e.g.*). Plants like *Sagittaria* and *Alisma* begin their development submersed, but most species of these genera become emergent for full growth and reproduction. Plants such as *Elodea*, although anchored in shallow water, do not emerge except to place their flowers at the surface. Some species of *Myriophyllum* are highly sensitive to intense light (even when under water where light is relatively weak), whereas others must grow so as to obtain maximum illumination. Some plants develop red, anthocyan pigments apparently in response to strong light.

It is clear, therefore, that aquatic plants require the same ecological conditions, and must meet the same problems for survival as do terrestrial. But there are differences in degree or prevalence. Water, for example, becomes a critical problem for land plants which aquatic plants are spared. Gases, especially oxygen for respiration and carbon dioxide for photosynthesis, abundant in the atmosphere, are in minimum supply in the aquatic medium. Light intensity and duration are not so much of a problem for land plants as for aquatic. Temperature ranges and rate of temperature change are relatively a low-level problem for aquatic plants, whereas land plants must adjust to a great range in temperature levels and to very sudden variations. The adjustment that aquatic plants are capable of making to environmental factors are well-illustrated in their biology and morphology, and in turn these are responsible for their distribution and zonation. Some of the ecological factors and responses to them are:

1. Light. Critical for photosynthesis and in some instances for seed germination.

Much of the light that reaches the surface of water is reflected (as much as 75%

3

from a ruffled surface) and the amount which does penetrate becomes scattered and absorbed as it passes through the water. Hence only a small percentage is available for photosynthesis. Compensation for this is reached by submersed plants having relatively numerous and small or finely dissected leaves. Another fortuitous character of many aquatic plants (Nymphaceae, Water Lily Family) and species of *Potamogeton*) is seen in the length of petioles and the length of stem internodes, thus placing blades in a suitable light zone. In a lake one on shore may locate the 12-foot depth by the inner margin of a water lily zone. It has been estimated that a photosynthetic day (varies with time of year) in northern latitudes (40°-55° L.) at a depth of about 45 feet is from 11:45 A.M. to 12:15 P.M. so great the angle of incidence and the amount of light reaching that depth.

2. Gases. Critical for oxidation, for photosynthesis and for buoyancy.

Most submersed plants have tissues well-supplied with canals, lacunae and gas-storing chambers. As for the obtaining of sufficient light, submersed leaves are ordinarily small or finely dissected and numerous. In some genera there are emergent species which have finely divided or narrow leaves below the water level, but flat blades above (*Ranunculus* spp. *e.g.*). *Oenone*, which demands well-aerated water, has tufts of hairs on the leaf surface which facilitate the absorption of gases.

3. Nutrients and Essential Elements.

These are in solution for aquatic plants; the plant is bathed in a culture solution. Hence obtaining nutrients is less of a problem for aquatic plants than for land plants where only the root system is bathed in a solution. Accordingly, the circulation (transport system), as might be expected is less developed in aquatic plants and morphologically the aquatic plant has weakly developed xylem and phloem tissues.

4. Currents and Mechanical Disturbance.

Physical disturbances (currents, ice, etc.) present problems to which aquatic plants make adjustment by having practically no reinforced or mechanical supporting tissues, remaining limp so as to bend with water currents. Land plants in an atmospheric medium must have highly specialized tissues resulting in rigidity. Hence one does not find well-developed sclerenchyma and collenchyma nor bark in aquatic plants.

5. Reproduction.

Whereas land plants have the use of wind, insects and gravity for achieving pollination and seed dispersal, aquatic plants must rely almost entirely on water or water currents. This accounts for many special and highly refined habits and structures different from those employed by terrestrial plants. Seed-production is not nearly as assured for the aquatic plant and by and large aquatic plants resort to vegetative means for reproduction. Branch pieces are easily regenerative and rhizomes proliferate readily, forming extensive beds of the same species. Obviously seed dispersal is facile for aquatic plants when compared with land plants which have many structural and functional devices to achieve dispersal.

Zonation

As previously mentioned, the demands of aquatic plant species and their ability to adjust determine zonation. Representative zones; and typical species are:

I. Deep Water (10-12 feet)
   Nuphar advena, N. variegata
   Nymphaea odorata, N. tuberosa
   Potamogeton praelongus, P. illinoisensis
   Vallisneria americana

II. Shallow Water (3-5-7 feet)
   Isoetes occidentalis
   Marsilea uncinata
   Equisetum fluviatile

Elodea canadensis, E. occidentalis, E. densa
Potamogeton, many spp., *P. natans, P. gramineus, P. epihydrus*
Glyceria striata
Scirpus validus
Ceratophyllum demersum (Floating)
Myriophyllum exalbescens, M. heterophyllum
Polygonum natans
Ranunculus circinatus
Utricularia vulgaris, U. intermedia

III. Shallow, shore water zone (6 Inches-2 Feet). (Mostly emergent plants)
Alisma plantago-aquatica
Pontederia cordata
Sagittaria latifolia
Scirpus americana
Naias flexilia
Heteranthera dubia
Potamogeton filiformis
Polygonum natans, P. hydropiperoides
Hippuris vulgaris
Ranunculus flabellaris, R. flammula

IV. Marginal (Moist to Wet; Bogs and Marshes).
Equisetum scirpoides, E. litorale

Isoetes butleri, I. eatoni, I. melanopoda
Carex aurea, C. lanuginosa, C. stipata and many other spp.
Eleocharis acicularis, E. minima, E. rostellata
Juncus spp.
Eriocaulon decangulare, E. septangulare
Xyris ambigua, X. caroliniana
Typha latifolia, T. angustifolia
Polygonum punctatum
Myaca aubletii
Ranunculus flammula
Potentilla anserina, P. palustris
Ludwigia spp.
Salix spp.
Alnus spp.
Cephalanthus occidentalis

V. Free-floating Plants
Ricciocarpus natans
Riccia fluitans
Azolla caroliniana
Salvinia rotundifolia
Ceratopteris pteridoides
Lemna minor, L. perpusilla, L. trisulca
Spirodela polyrhiza
Pistia stratiotes
Eichhornia crassipes

Collecting Aquatic Plants

Aquatic plants which are deeply submersed must be collected by a raking tool, or by an especially constructed "plant hook." Such a tool can be made very simply by running 3 or 4 double strands of heavy wire through a 10-inch section of 1½-inch pipe. The doubled strands should be about 2 feet long. The loops of the doubled strands are twisted together to form an eye-hole. The free ends of the wire are then bent back to form an anchor-like hook. A small amount of solder or melted lead can be poured into the pipe to keep the wires in position and to give weight to the hook. In the twisted knot of wires a small but strong rope or heavy cord is tied, about 35 to 40 feet usually being suitable (depending upon the depth of water to be sampled). The plant hook is tossed from shore or from a boat and dragged along the bottom to grapple the plants. Specimens can be carried to the laboratory in pails or tubs. A simple method is to use ordinary plastic bags (food bags in rolls obtained at the grocery store are ideal). Small collections or individual specimens can be kept fresh and unbroken for quite some time when placed in such bags with just enough water to bathe the roots and to maintain suitable humidity.

It is often desirable to examine plants in the field to determine flower and fruit characters, stipules, etc. For this a 14 × or 20 × doublet handlens is needed. The collector is reminded to have the handlens safely tied around the neck and to have the plant hook affixed to the boat when working over water.

Either before or after making identification of plants they may be prepared as herbarium specimens. Erect and/or firm plants may be placed in folded newspaper and plant driers as are terrestrial species. Submersed plants and those with flexible, drooping, tangled and highly divided leaves are best cared for by placing them directly on herbarium paper under water. For this 12 x 18-inch baking pans are suitable. The specimen is first rinsed and washed of extraneous material and dead leaves. Then it is placed in a pan of clean water. A sheet of herbarium paper supported on a 11 x 15-inch sheet of zinc or firm aluminum can then be slipped under the specimen. With tweezers and needles the specimen can be floated and spread on the paper in a life-like position, the various parts being arranged so as to show taxonomic features clearly. The metal sheet and its paper can then be slowly removed by sliding it back and up out of the water and placed in a semi-vertical position to drain.

After all excess water has been drained away the sheet with its specimen can then be placed in a folded newspaper. The newspaper is placed between blotters and ventilators and put to press. If the specimen is especially wet, or thick and matted, a small sheet of muslin can be laid over the plant. Plants with especially thick stems and dense root masses should be split or divided. Also, large flowers such as the yellow water lily (*Nuphar*) should be halved for the press in addition to an uncut flower. If specimens are mucilaginous a sheet of transparent plastic can be used to prevent sticking.

It may be desirable or of interest to collect dry fruits and/or seeds to be used in identification and comparison of specimens used as food by birds and other animals. After drying, seeds are packaged in small envelopes and can be filed, or affixed to the herbarium sheet.

What Is a Species?

By way of explanation for the inexperienced reader, a species is a population of organisms which are similar or identical. Thus, one of the yellow water lilies is an example of a species and all similar water lilies bear the specific epithet *advena*, for example. There are other yellow water lilies which are in general similar but which consistently vary enough to be recognizably different and so are called by another specific name, *variegata*, for example. The yellow water lilies which have much in common are apparently related and they are included together to constitute a genus, *Nuphar*. Thus we have *Nuphar advena*, *N. variegata*, *N. polysepala* and others. The genus and species name together constitute the scientific name of an organism; thus we have the binomial system of nomenclature.

We have in the same pond perhaps water lilies which seem to have much in common with the yellow water lily (such as general stem and leaf characters and embryo anatomy) but which are clearly not the same in outstanding respects such as shape of flower, number of petals, form of fruit, etc. There are several species of white or lotus-like water lilies which comprise the genus *Nymphaea* such as *N. odorata*, *N. tuberosa*, etc. *Nymphaea* and *Nuphar* are obviously related so these two genera (with all their species) and other genera with somewhat similar characteristics are grouped into a family, the Nymphaeaceae. Here would be classed *Nelumbo*, the yellow lotus, and *Brasenia*, the water shield, and others. Families of organisms which have some characteristics in common are often grouped to form Orders, the Orders comprise Classes and Classes comprise Phyla or Divisions. The botanist refers to these groupings (species, genus, etc.) as taxa (singular taxon).

How to Use the Key

The following key is the dichotomous type, that is, two choices are presented and one must decide which of the statements applies to a specimen in question. Having made a selection, one follows the numbers through the succeeding choices, eventually arriving at a genus name. If one does not reach a satisfactory conclusion it is necessary to return to a previously considered dichotomy which offers some alternatives and follow through on another series of choices. In a number of instances the key leads to the same genus name in more than one place. This is necessary because the genus may include species which are variable in respect to a character used in the key statements. It will be noted that in so far as possible vegetative characters are used in presenting choices. When final separation cannot be concluded by using these characters, flower and/or reproductive features are employed in the key. Characteristics which must be considered are:

1. Whether true leaves and stem are present.
2. Leaf shape.
3. Type of leaf margin.
4. Whether the leaf is simple or compound.
5. Arrangement of leaves on the stem.
6. Presence of ligule.
7. Presence of stipules.
8. Presence of sheaths (some leaves occur only as sheaths at the base of the stem).
9. Form of flowers. (See text figures 1-5 illustrating some flower types.)
10. Arrangement and location of flowers; type of inflorescence.

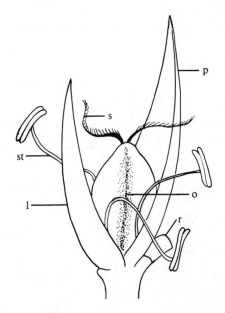

Plate 1   Diagram of a grass flower. l, Lemma; o, Ovary; p, Palea; r, Rachilla; s, Stigma; st, Stamen.

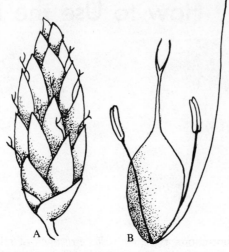

Plate 3 Inflorescence of the Cyperaceae, diagrammatic. A, Spikelet; B, Perfect flower with pistil and stamens.

Plate 2 Diagram of a grass spikelet. g, Glumes.

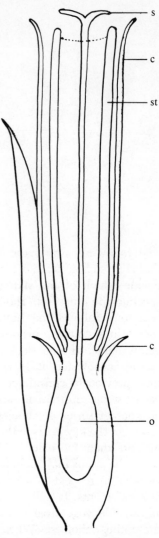

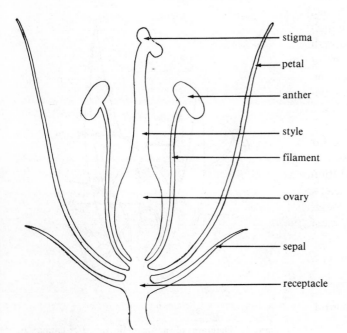

stigma

petal

anther

style

filament

ovary

sepal

receptacle

Plate 4 Diagram of flower in the Compositae. C, (above), corolla; C, (below), calyx; O, ovary; S. stigma; st, stamen.

Plate 5 Diagram of typical complete flower.

General References

Arber, Agnes. 1920. Water Plants. (Reprinted 1963 by J. Cramer.) Weinheim.

Benson, Lyman. 1957. Plant Classification. Heath & Co. Boston.

Cornell, D. S. and Cornell, Helen B. 1975. Aquatic and Wetland Plants of Southwestern United States. Vols. I, II. Stanford University Press. Stanford, Calif.

Daubs, E. H. 1965. A Monograph of Lemnaceae. University Illinois Press. Urbana.

Fassett, F. N. 1940. A manual of aquatic plants. McGraw-Hill Book Co. New York. (Reprinted 1966 by University of Wisconsin Press with Appendix by E. C. Ogden). Madison.

Fernald, M. L. 1950. Gray's Manual of Botany. American Book Co. New York.

Gleason, H. A. and Cronquist, A. 1963. Manual of Vascular Plants of Northeastern United States and Adjacent Canada. Van Nostrand Co. New York.

Marie-Victorin, Frère. Flore Laurentienne. Montréal, Canada.

Martin, A. C. and Uhler, F. M. 1951. Food of Game Ducks in the United States and Canada. U.S.D.A. Technical Bull. No. 634.

1939. (Reprinted as Research Report No. 30, Fish & Wildlife Service, U.S. Dept. Interior, 1951.)

Martin, A. C., Zim, H. E. and Nelson, A. L. 1951. American Wildlife and Plants. McGraw-Hill Book Co. New York.

Mason, H. L. 1957. A Flora of the Marshes of California. University of California Press. Berkeley.

Mohlenbrock, R. H. 1976. Sedges. *Cyperus* to *Scleria*. The Illustrated Flora of Illinois. Southern Illinois University Press. Carbondale, Ill.

Muenscher, W. C. 1944. Aquatic plants of the United States. Comstock. Ithaca, New York.

Peck, M. E. 1941. A Manual of the Higher Plants of Oregon. Binfords and Mort. Portland, Ore.

Sculthorpe, C. D. 1967. The Biology of Aquatic Vascular Plants. St. Martin's Press. New York.

Steward, A. N., Dennis, L. J., and Gilkey, Helen M. 1963. Aquatic Plants of the Pacific Northwest. Oregon State University Press. Corvallis.

Key to the Genera of Aquatic Plants

1a   Plants with true leaves, or true stem and (usually) roots; floating or rooted; aquatic, or on shore 23

1b   Plants without true leaves, stem and roots (although rootlets are present on some thalloid duckweeds); plants with small (2 to 8 mm long) "leaves" as in the mosses, *e.g.*; a lobed thallus as in the liverworts; or plants filamentous 2

2a   Plants thalloid, sometimes dichotomously lobed (liverworts); plants with joints or flat lobes, or minute globular thalli (duckweeds); plants without an elongate axis with branches or scales (See, however, *Dermatocarpon*, a thalloid, aquatic lichen not included here) 3

2b   Plants otherwise; filamentous (algae), or with elongate axes bearing small, scalelike "leaves" (mosses) 10

3a   Plants floating (sometimes incidentally stranded on mud); rootlets present or absent 5

3b   Plants attached, growing on moist substrates, with rhizoids forming a mat along a midrib on the ventral side 4

4a   Thallus a lobed, flattened, dorsiventral, leaflike expansion, with saucerlike gemmae cups on the upper surface; when mature, with sex organs borne on stalked gametophores which are disclike (male) or palm treelike (female) arising from notches in the thallus (Liverworts). Fig. 1 .... *Marchantia*

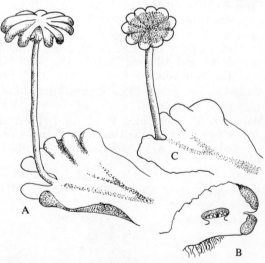

Figure 1

Figure 1 *Marchantia polymorpha* (Marchantiaceae) A. Portion of thallus showing an archegoniophore (female branch); B. A young thallus with cupule and gemmae buds; C. Portion of a thallus with antheridiophore (male branch).

This liverwort is dioecious, that is the female and male reproductive organs are borne on separate plants. Before maturity the plants bear small cups on the dorsal surface in which special regenerative buds (gemmae) are produced. *Marchantia* is found on stream banks, on logs and rocks, or in swamp margins. It is a pioneer on denuded soils or on ash after a bog fire. The species shown here is nearly world-wide in its distribution.

4b **Thallus a flattened, leaflike expanse without saucerlike gemmae cups; when mature with a stalked, female gametophore distinctly coneshaped at the apex. Fig. 2** .... *Conocephalum*

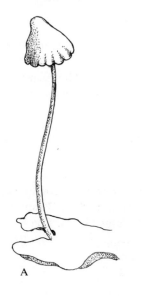

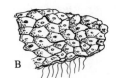

Figure 2

Figure 2 *Conocephalum conicum* (Marchantiaceae) A. Portion of thallus showing an archegoniophore (female branch) with its cone-shaped head on the under side of which archegonia are produced; B. Portion of thallus showing the raised areolae in which there is a breathing pore.

Plants occur in much the same habitat as *Marchantia;* differ in the prominence of the areolae on the dorsal surface, and in the shape of the disc which bears the archegonia, being conical rather than disclike. Also this genus lacks the cupules and gemmae buds. *Conocephalum* has a faint spicy odor.

5a (3) **Plants without rootlets** **7**

5b **Plants with rootlets** **6**

6a **Thallus composed of 2 or a few, circular joints, up to 3.5 mm wide, which are purple on the under side, the joints showing about 7 indistinct nerves, with several rootlets from each joint (Great Duckweed). Fig. 3** .... *Spirodela*

Figure 3

Figure 3 *Spirodela polyrhiza* (Lemnaceae) Habit showing a variety of shapes of joints. Note the several rootlets borne on each joint.

This duckweed is the largest in the Lemnaceae. It forms surface "meadows" in quiet water and is readily identified by the purple underside of the lobes and by the numerous rootlets. *Spirodela* is important as a wild fowl food plant and often is so abundant as to become a nuisance.

6b   **Thallus composed of oval, circular, or elongate-forked joints, 2 to 4 mm across, with 1 to 3 radiating nerves, not purple on the under side, with only 1 rootlet from each joint (Duckweed). Fig. 4 ......**
.. *Lemna*

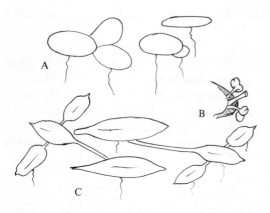

Figure 4

Figure 4 *Lemna* (Lemnaceae) A. *Lemna minor;* B. Marginal flower of *Lemna minor;* C. *Lemna trisculca.*

This genus is perhaps the most common and abundant of all the duckweeds, especially *L. minor* which forms extensive surface mats in quiet waters and in slowly flowing streams. It is a useful index organism of hardwater habitats. The plants proliferate rapidly by budding and often present a nuisance. *L. val-*

diviana has oblong rather than oval joints. *L. trisculca* has spatulate joints that form T-shaped or cross-shaped arrangements. The plants float in tangled clumps beneath the surface. Each joint of *Lemna* bears a single, threadlike rootlet.

7a   **(5) Plants formed of one or more minute, elongate, bandlike or flattened thalli 4 to 8 mm long, arranged in a star-shaped cluster, the cluster usually floating just beneath water surface (Strap-shaped Duckweed). Fig. 5 .... *Wolffiella***

Figure 5

Figure 5 *Wolffiella floridana* (Lemnaceae) Habit.

This curiously-shaped plant has a fingerlike or strap-shaped thallus that often occurs in stellate clusters; has no rootlets. The plant is widely distributed in eastern and southern United States.

7b   **Thalli shaped otherwise 8**

8a   **Plants composed of minute globules, or subspherical, granular bodies, 2 mm or less in diameter (Water Meal). Fig. 6 ....**
.. *Wolffia*

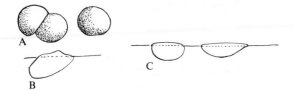

Figure 6

Figure 6 *Wolffia* (Lemnaceae) A. *Wolffia columbiana;* B. *Wolffia papulifera;* C. *Wolffia punctata.*

The minute thalli in this genus are the smallest flowering plants in the world. They occur as green grains at or near the surface of quiet waters. Tiny flowers are borne on the margins of the grains. These species are probably more widely distributed than indicated by present records because they are so easily overlooked in aquatic situations, intermingled as they are with other species of Lemnaceae and with *Ricciocarpus natans*. *Wolffia punctata* is the most commonly found. The thallus is flattened on the under side; has dark spots.

8b   Thalli shaped otherwise **9**

9a   Thallus, a narrow, flattened dichotomously lobed ribbon, often with a few white rhizoids from the ventral surface (Liverworts). Fig. 7 .... *Riccia*

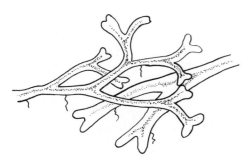

Figure 7

Figure 7 *Riccia fluitans* (Ricciaceae).

This thalloid liverwort may be either aquatic or epiphytic on trees in humid forests (especially in the tropics). Species may also occur on logs and fallen wood in northern latitudes. *Riccia fluitans* is a dichotomously divided ribbon; occurs in clumps in marginal waters of lakes and sloughs. There are few or no rhizoids. The plants are useful as duck food; are widely distributed.

9b   Thallus lumpy, or moundlike, with dichotomously lobed margins; numerous, dark purple scales from the ventral surface (Liverwort) Fig. 8 ....
.... *Ricciocarpus*

Figure 8

Figure 8 *Ricciocarpus natans* (Ricciaceae) A. Vertical view of a thallus; B. Lateral view showing ventral scales.

This species is mostly aquatic and floating but may be found stranded on mud. The dichotomously lobed mounds are grooved above and have dark-colored, purplish scales from the lower surface. The plants may be abundant in favorable, quiet habitats and become important in aquatic biology, especially as food for birds.

10a (2) Thalli filamentous stalks, thread-like; branching usually very evident 11

10b Thalli with leaflike lobes or joints, or with small (3 to 8 mm long) scalelike "leaves" arranged along a "stem" (Mosses). 15

11a Main filament somewhat rigid; plants growing erect or spreading from the bottom of aquatic habitats, with branches at definite nodes; plants macroscopic, 3 cm to as much as 1 M in length 12

11b Thalli with limp, lax axes 14

12a Plants gray-green (usually) because of lime deposits (gritty to the touch), with a skunk-like odor; most species with axes enclosed by overlying, cortical or columnar cells (seen with a hand lens); nodes with whorls of branches ("leaves") all the same length (Chlorophyta; Muskgrass, Stonewort) Fig. 9 .... *Chara*

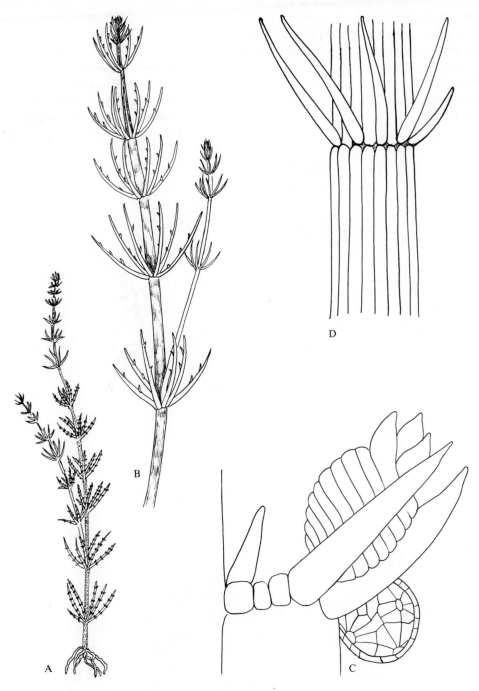

Figure 9

Figure 9 *Chara* sp. (Characeae) A. Habit of plant showing whorls of short branches at the nodes, and the basal rhizoids; B. Anterior portion of a plant showing short branches of limited growth and one branch with unlimited growth; C. A node of a branch on which an oogonium (nucule) and an antheridium (globule) are borne; D. Section of a "stem" showing cortical cells.

12b Plants without lime, usually dark green; without a disagreeable odor; no overlying cortical cells 13

13a Branches, especially those bearing reproductive structures dichotomously or trichotomously forked at the tips; branches of uniform length, in whorls at the nodes. Fig. 10 .... *Nitella*

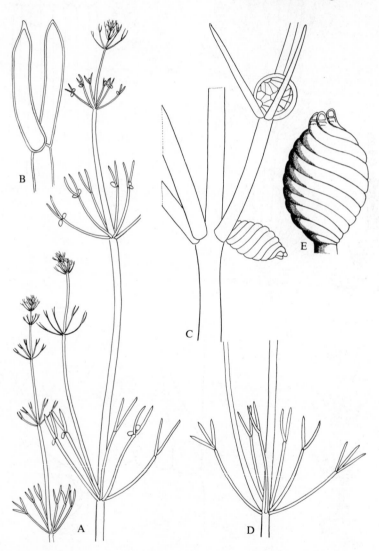

Figure 10

Members of this genus are more delicate and greener than *Chara* often is, and have no disagreeable odor. Plants are uncorticated and do not deposit lime on the exterior. They usually occur in soft water with a low pH. Many species are translucent.

Figure 10 *Nitella* sp. (Characeae) A. Habit of anterior portion of thallus showing bifurcations at the tips of the branches; B. Cells at the apex of a branch; C. A section of a branch with an oogonium (nucule) below and an antheridium above, borne vertically in the furcations; D. A species with trifurcate branch tips; E. Oogonium with 10 cells in the coronula.

13b Branches not divided or forked at the tip; some branches at the nodes short, others much elongated and threadlike; reproductive structures in heads of short branches. Fig. 11 .... *Tolypella*

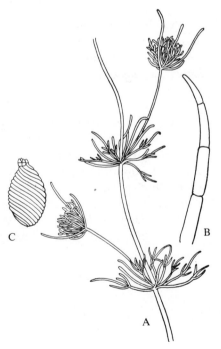

Figure 11 *Tolypella* (Characeae) A. Habit of plant portion showing the rather dense heads of short branches on which the sex organs are produced; B. Tip of a branch; C. An oogonium showing the divisions of the cells in the coronula.

This is a relative of *Nitella*, with but a few species and more limited in distribution. *Tolypella* can be identified by its scraggly appearance resulting from the irregular branch lengths, some being very long and threadlike. Numerous short branches form clumps in which the reproductive structures are borne. Species may be either dioecious or monoecious.

14a (11) Thallus arbuscular (treelike), embedded in soft, amorphous mucilage, with whorls of branches at definite nodes, producing a "beaded" effect; plants gray-violet, tawny or buff-colored, (Rhodophyta). Fig. 12 ....
.... *Batrachospermum*

Figure 11

Figure 12

Figure 12 *Batrachospermum* (Batrachospermaceae) A. Habit of anterior portion of plant showing beaded effect produced by whorls of short branches at nodes; B. Branch tip showing pyriform cells and apical hairs; C. A carpogonial branch with a spermatium fused with the trichogyne of the carpogonium; vegetative branches from the lower cells of the carpogonial branch; D. Apices of branches bearing spermatangia.

This fresh-water red alga forms highly gelatinized, bushy tufts in either flowing water or in pools. There is very little phycoerythrin hence the plants are gray-green, violet-green or tawny. Large specimens in the tropics may be two feet in length, but usually the thallus is a short, tufted growth on rocks and sticks. Whorls of branches give a beaded effect, reminding one of strings of frog eggs, hence the name *Batracho* (frog) *Sperm* (seeds).

14b Thallus a tuft of repeatedly branched filaments, forming a bushy growth, without whorls of out-turned branches; not embedded in mucilage; plants green (Chlorophyta). Fig. 13 ...... *Cladophora*

Figure 13

Figure 13 *Cladophora glomerata* (Cladophoraceae). Habit of anterior portion of branched filament; cells with netlike or fragmented chloroplast.

This genus occurs mostly as a bushy tufted green alga, attached to rocks and wood in flowing water, on dams and in waterfalls. But some species are found abundantly in lakes, especially on wave-washed shores. Growth is profuse in hardwater situations and when plants become free-floating they may cause considerable nuisance when they are washed onto beaches as tangled, decaying, ropy masses.

15a (10) Thallus attached, terrestrial or submersed, with small, leaf-like scales or lobes arranged along a short or long "stem" plants sometimes becoming disattached (Mosses) 16

15b Thallus floating, with round, oval or elongate joints or leaflike lobes, not arranged on an elongate "stem" (Water Ferns; Lemnaceae) 20

16a Plants in bogs, green or pale green (sometimes tipped with red); stems erect with radially arranged branches which are closely clustered near the top where they form a rosette; stem and branches (some drooping) clothed by small, overlapping "leaves" (Bog Moss). Fig. 14 .... *Sphagnum*

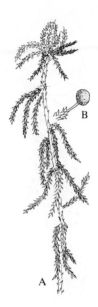

Figure 14

Figure 14 *Sphagnum* (Sphagnaceae) A. Habit of upper portion of a gametophore showing decurrent and upwardly directed branches; B. A mature sporophyte at the tip of a branch.

This is the familiar bog moss, often light green because most of the plant body is composed of empty, colorless cells. Species may occur on margins of softwater lakes, in acid soils and in meadows, sometimes at high altitudes if there is an abundance of moisture. Also *Sphagnum* may form mats around the margins of hard-water, calcareous lakes contributing to the "quaking bog" that encroaches on the lake. Species are differentiated by details of leaf morphology. Some such as *S. magellanicum* and *S. rubellum* are reddish in the upper branches. This moss is economically important as peat, as a packing material, as a conditioner for horticultural soils and in the preparation of surgical bandages.

16b   Plants not as above **17**

17a   Thallus prostrate, composed of an axis with deep, lateral lobings which nearly form leaflike expansions; plants mostly terrestrial in moist habitats (Leafy Liverwort). Fig. 15 .... *Chiloscyphus*

Figure 15

Figure 15 *Chiloscyphus* (Harpanthaceae) Portion of a prostrate thallus.

This liverwort has a thallus in which a branched axis gives rise bilaterally to deep lobes which are leaflike; belongs to the Leafy Liverworts of the Jungermanniales. Plants are found on stones in cold, running water.

17b   Thallus otherwise; plants aquatic **18**

18a   "Leaves" forming three rows along the "stem," closely overlapping, without a midrib (Moss). Fig. 16 .... *Fontinalis*

Figure 16

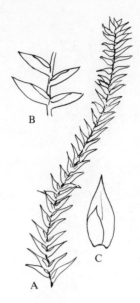

Figure 17

Figure 16 *Fontinalis* (Fontinalaceae) A. Anterior portion of a branch with closely overlapping, rather rigid leaves; B. Leaves with dorsal keel; C. Single leaves.

There are several species of this moss (Bryales) which are aquatic. *F. antipyretica* is perhaps the most common, a dark green and relatively large species, occurring on rocks in swiftly running water. The leaves are somewhat trough-shaped, closely overlapping, have no midrib. Such mosses are of biological significance since they harbor aquatic insects, larvae and other microbiota.

18b "Leaves" spreading and curled, either in 2 rows along the "stem" or spiral 19

19a "Leaves" in 2 rows spreading from two sides of the "stem," with a midrib and a secondary small plate of cells forming a lateral pocket at the base (Moss). Fig. 17 .... *Fissidens*

Figure 17 *Fissidens* (Fissidentaceae) A. Anterior portion of a branch showing leaves arranged on two sides; B. Leaf arrangement; C. Single leaf showing the secondary flap of cells at the base.

This is a sprawling moss with elongate-elliptic leaves that spread from two sides of the stem. There is a midrib and a plate of superficial cells on one side at the base. Several species occur in both lakes and streams, attached to and covering rocks and twigs.

19b "Leaves" spirally arranged, arising from 3 sides of the "stem," with a midrib (Moss). Fig. 18 .... *Drepanocladus*

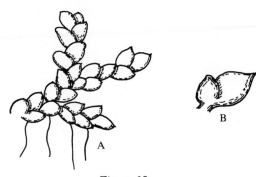

Figure 19

Figure 18

Figure 18 *Drepanocladus* (Hypnaceae) **A.** A branch showing curling lateral branches; **B.** A single leaf showing sickle shape.

In this genus the leaves are spirally arranged, curled, and have a midrib. Species usually grow profusely, forming dense mats on submersed wood, on lake bottoms, sometimes floating in extensive clumps. Biologically they are important as oxygenators and as primary producers in lakes which cannot support aquatic vegetation, especially soft-water lakes low in nutrients.

20a (15) **Leaves small, (3 to 4 mm) smooth, oval, closely arranged on a short stem, each leaf having a ventral lobe that bears a sporocarp when mature; leaves usually tinged with red (Water Velvet, and aquatic fern). Fig. 19** .... *Azolla*

Figure 19 *Azolla* (Salviniaceae) **A.** Thallus with small overlapping leaves and rootlets; **B.** Single leaf showing thumblike ventral lobe.

This is called Water Velvet, a small, aquatic fern which grows so densely as to form surface mats, often tinged with red. The plant has a short stem giving rise bilaterally to rows of overlapping, scalelike leaves that have a ventral, submersed lobe. *A. caroliniana* is the common species in North America; is biologically important as food for aquatic birds.

20b Plants otherwise **21**

21a Leaves circular, bilobed, 2 or 4 from a short stem and bearing stiff bristles on the upper surface; lower submersed leaves finely dissected, appearing like roots, bearing sporocarps; roots lacking (Water Fern; Floating Moss). Fig. 20 .... *Salvinia*

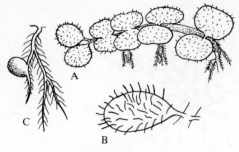

Figure 20

Figure 20 *Salvinia* (Salviniaceae) A. A portion of a stem showing circular floating, dorsal leaves and the finely divided, submersed ventral leaves; B. A single leaf blade with stiff trichomes; C. Ventral leaf with a sporocarp.

Whereas some tropical species of this genus of aquatic fern may have larger leaves, those which occur in the United States have leaves 1 to 1.5 cm across when mature. Besides the two rows of dorsal leaves there are finely dissected ventral and submersed leaves that have the appearance of roots, but the plant has no roots. The leaves arise 3 at a node. In the tropics, species of *Salvinia* may become so dense as to clog barge canals and to interfere with navigation. *Salvinia* is much-used as an aquarium plant.

21b   Plants otherwise **22**

22a   Thallus with a pair of floating, leaflike lobes, purple on the under side, with several roots from each lobe or joint (Great Duckweed). Fig. 3 .... *Spirodela*

22b   Thallus with oval, rounded or spatula-shaped lobes or joints, with 1 rootlet per joint; thallus not purple on the under side. Fig. 4 .... *Lemna*

23a   (1) Plants semi-woody vines, woody shrubs or trees; semi-aquatic **24**

23b   Plants herbaceous, annual or perennial, sometimes with persistent, semi-woody stems **36**

24a   Leaves needlelike; coniferous trees with deciduous leaves (*) **25**

24b   Leaves broad, with or without a petiole **26**

25a   Needles angular in cross section, several in a cluster or fascicle (Larch, Tamarack). Fig. 21 .... *Larix*

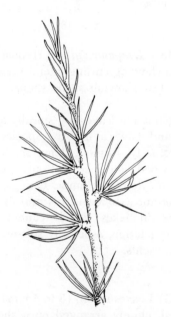

Figure 21

(*) *Picea mariana* or Black Spruce (evergreen) has leaves borne singly from all sides of the stem. The needles are angular in cross section and stiff. Dwarfed trees grow in northern bogs often with Tamarack and associated plants.

Figure 21 *Larix laricina* (Pinaceae) Twig showing fascicled, needlelike leaves.

Although not usually thought of as an aquatic plant tamarack or larch occurs in bogs and acid situation along with *Sphagnum,* cranberry, leather-leaf, pitcher plants and sundew. The trees, usually not more than 25 or 30 feet high, have soft needlelike leaves in fascicles which become yellow and drop away each fall.

25b **Needles flat, borne singly from two sides of the stem; twigs flat (Bald Cypress). Fig. 22** .... *Taxodium*

Figure 22 *Taxodium distichum* (Taxodiaceae) A. Twig, leaf shape and arrangement; B. Carpellate cone.

Bald Cypress is an inhabitor of swamps in southeastern United States where there are extensive, but rapidly disappearing stands. It is more nearly an aquatic than *Larix* because the trees grow in the water of swamps and river margins, sending up the familiar cypress knees which supposedly facilitate oxygen uptake. Galls develop on the twigs and these, falling into the water, are used by aquatic birds for food.

26a **(24) Plants with semi-woody stems; perennial** **27**

26b **Plants definitely woody; trees and shrubs** **29**

27a **Plant a creeping vine in *Sphagnum* bogs or in peaty soil (Cranberry). Fig. 23** .... ***Vaccinium***

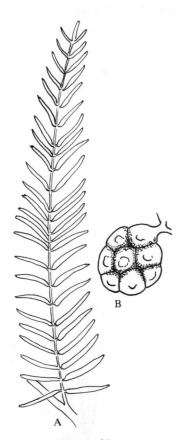

Figure 22

Figure 23

Figure 23 *Vaccinium oxycoccus* (Ericaceae). Portion of procumbent stem with a flower.

Cranberry is a creeping, semi-woody vine inhabiting *Sphagnum* bogs, or as *V. macrocarpon* is grown commercially in acid soil. Like many other members of the Ericaceae species are confined to acid situations.

27b Plants erect **28**

28a Stems semi-woody, with a spongy base; leaves tapered at the base to a short petiole, opposite, but occasionally in 3's and rarely alternate on the same stem; plants marginal, the branches drooping and sprawling over the water (Water Willow). Fig. 24 .... *Decodon*

Figure 24 *Decodon verticillatum* (Lythraceae) A. Plant (stylized); B. Twig showing opposite leaves and whorls of flowers at the nodes.

Water Willow is important as a builder of lake margins. Dense stands sometimes occupy a marshy area, or there may be isolated clumps in shallow water of bays and lagoons.

28b Stems semi-woody or herbaceous, but not spongy at the base; leaves opposite, sessile (Sea Milkwort). Fig. 25 ....
.... *Glaux*

Figure 24

Figure 25

Figure 25 *Glaux maritima* (Primulaceae) A. Habit of plant; B. Single flower.

This is a perennial, semi-woody and profusely branched plant (when mature) which is confined to brackish tidal flats or to saline waters inland. It occurs on all coasts of continental United States. Flowers are solitary in the axils of linear or oval leaves and produce beaked capsules as fruits.

29a (26) **Leaves spirally arranged, arising from three sides of the stem** 30

29b **Leaves alternate or opposite** 31

30a **Leaves broadly oval or orbicular in outline, coarsely serrate on the margin; bud scales several (Alder). Fig. 26** .... *Alnus*

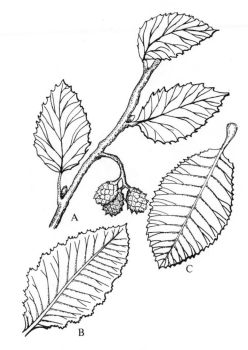

Figure 26

Figure 26 *Alnus* (Betulaceae) A. Twig of *A. crispa* with carpellate flowers; B. *A. incana* leaf; C. *A. crispa* leaf.

There are several species of Alder which form thickets along lake shores and stream courses. The trees are monoecious, the flowers occurring in catkins. The pistillate persist as dry cones.

30b **Leaves elongate and narrowly elliptic to nearly linear (rarely elongate-oval), usually with stipules (often deciduous); margins either finely or remotely serrate; bud scales 1; shrubs, marginal along stream courses and beaches (Willow). Fig. 27** .... *Salix*

Figure 27

32a **Leaves lanceolate (or nearly linear), revolute (rolled under along the margin), green above, decidedly whitened beneath (Swamp Laurel). Fig. 27A ......** .... *Kalmia*

Figure 27A

Figure 27 *Salix* (Salicaceae) A. Twig with staminate catkin; B. Scale with pistil; C. Scale with stamens; D. Leaf of *S. serissima*.

There are numerous species of willow, given the ancient Celtic name "Salis" which means "near the water." Many are important as beach-builders and can be used in erosion control. The wood is used for making charcoal in some sections, and twigs are used in basket-making. Species are differentiated by morphological details of the flowers and leaves.

31a (29) Leaves opposite 32

31b Leaves alternate 34

Figure 27A *Kalmia* (Ericaceae) A. *K. angustifolia* twig showing opposite, elliptical leaves and a few saucer-shaped (pink or white) flowers; B. *K. polifolia* leaf showing enrolled margins.

This is the Swamp Laurel or Bog Wintergreen growing characteristically in *Sphagnum* bogs. Plants are low shrubs from 30 cm to nearly waist high. *Kalmia* is associated with *Ledum* (Labrador Tea) and with *Chamaedaphne* (Leather Leaf) and other members of the heath family. *K. polifolia* with enrolled leaf margins is perhaps the more common and widely distributed species. The showy pink or white flowers occur in terminal racemes.

In *K. angustifolia* the flowers are lateral, solitary or a few together.

32b Leaves otherwise 33

33a Leaves with several prominent veins, seen especially on the under side, curving boldly upward and outward from the midrib to the leaf margin which is slightly undulate, hairy on the under side; bark of stem red (Dogwood; Red Ozier Dogwood). Fig. 28 ....
.... ***Cornus stolonifera***

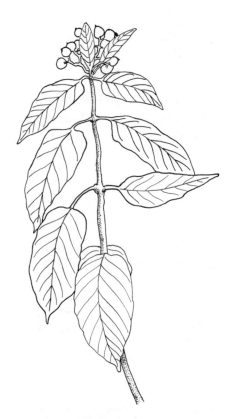

Figure 28

Figure 28 *Cornus stolonifera* (Cornaceae). Twig showing terminal clump of berrylike fruits (white).

This is the common and widely distributed Red Ozier Dogwood. The shrub has umbels of small, white flowers which produce clusters of white berrylike fruits. This species is conspicuous about swamps, stream courses and lake shores in winter because of the showy red bark. Other *Cornus* species with gray or slightly red (purplish) bark (*C. Amomum*) may occur in the same habitat, the latter having pubescent twigs and leaves. Apparently hybridization occurs among *Cornus* species and characters vary, especially bark color.

33b Lateral veins conspicuous but not so prominent on the lower surface, ending in a network at the margins which are entire; bark not reddish; leaves rarely occurring in 3's as well as opposite (Button Bush). Fig. 29 .... ***Cephalanthus***

Figure 29

Figure 29 *Cephalanthus occidentalis* (Rubiaceae). Twig with a terminal cluster of flowers and a mature, ball-like cluster of fruits.

This is the only shrub in the United States (native) belonging to the quinine family which is common in the tropics. The common name is derived from the headlike cluster of pyramidal fruits terminal on a long flower stalk. The shrubs occur marginally with Dogwood and Willows.

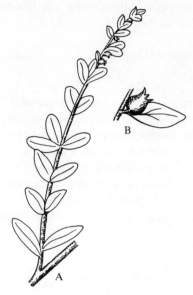

Figure 30

Figure 30 *Chamaedaphne calyculata* (Ericaceae) A. Twig showing leaf arrangement; B. Flower in axil of leaf.

Chamaedaphne forms dense thickets in *Sphagnum* bogs and in moist sandy soil. It is instrumental in the encroachment of a bog mat into a lake.

34a (31) Leaves broadly elliptic, with lateral veins very prominent as seen from the under side, curving upward and outward to the margins, not hairy on the underside; flowers small, in dense clusters; bark not reddish; shrubs of somewhat dry situations but sometimes occurring with *Cornus stolonifera* near aquatic habitats (Dogwood). Fig. 28 .... *Cornus* (p.p.)

34b Leaves narrowly elliptic; without prominent veins showing on the under side; shrubs of acid bogs(°) 35

35a Leaves with brownish scales above and below, showing as brown dots on the upper surface; leaves coarsely or remotely serrate along the apical margin (Leather Leaf). Fig. 30 .... *Chamaedaphne*

35b Leaves pale or dark-green, without brownish scales, sometimes with dotlike glands or hairs, usually glabrous; leaf margins entire or finely serrate throughout (Blueberry; Cranberry). Fig. 23 .... *Vaccinium*

(°) See also *Ledum groenlandicum* (Labrador Tea), a shrub of bogs which has alternate, narrow leaves that are densely brown-woolly on the under side; the capsule elongate oval; also *Andromeda glaucophylla* (Bog Rosemary) that has revolute leaves (rolled under along the margins) and with flattened or depressed globular fruits.

36a (23) Leaves ribbonlike, grasslike, sword-like or linear, with parallel or subparallel margins, more than ten times the width in length; simple (but see *Podostemum*, Fig. 107); or plants having long, slender, naked stems (*Eleocharis*, Fig. 134, *e.g.*) with leaves reduced to sheaths at the base; bearing flowers and fruits at or near the apex (but see *Glaux*, Fig. 25) 232

36b Leaves otherwise, not long ribbons nor grasslike and swordlike 37

37a Leaves with a broad blade of various shapes, not more than ten times the width in length; leaves simple or compound and sometimes divided into linear or threadlike segments, leaves with or without a petiole 38

37b Leaves in the form of small scales or leaflike joints (Fig. 4), green or colorless bracts or scales, sometimes underground on horizonal stems and occurring as forked linear threads (*Utricularia* spp. Fig. 116); in some plants leaves reduced to a rim at the stem nodes 215

38a Leaves in the form of hollow tubes or pitchers; insect-catching plants 39

38b Leaves otherwise, variously shaped, elongate, spatulate, oval, elliptic or circular (at least in outline), or with sagittate blades; leaves with or without a petiole 40

39a Leaves tubelike, pitcher-shaped, open or covered by a raised "awning" or a simple hood which has no downward projecting bracts (Pitcher Plant). Fig. 31 .... *Sarracenia*

Figure 31

Figure 31 *Sarracenia purpurea* (Sarraceniaceae). Plant with a single flower.

This is the most common of the eastern pitcher plants. The liquid in the hollow leaf contains enzymes which digest the soft parts of insects captured. This is apparently the chief source of nitrogen in the plant's nutrition and metabolism. *S. drummondi* occurs in southern bogs, has an awning or lid over the opening of the "pitcher." The procumbent leaves and the solitary flower of *S. purpurea*, borne on a naked scape are purplish, hence the species name. The southern U.S. species is known as Trumpets. Pitcher plants usually occur in *Sphagnum* bogs and in acid situations, but unexplainably *S. purpurea* is found in old bogs which have become basic, growing in sedge meadows.

39b Leaves tubelike pitchers, hooded with an opening on its underside, bearing a persistent, forked, tonguelike bract (Pitcher Plant). Fig. 32 .... *Darlingtonia californica*

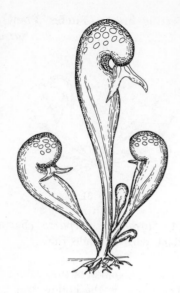

Figure 32

Figure 32 *Darlingtonia californica* (Sarraceniaceae). Plant with hooded leaves bearing forked bracts.

This is the only species of western pitcher plant. The leaves appear in clusters, straight and erect, with a hood over the opening and with a forked, tonguelike bract. Leaves vary in length from one or two inches when young to 30 inches when mature. The flowering scape is shorter than the leaves and bears a single, nodding, purple and yellow blossom. The species is mostly confined to coastal bogs of Oregon and northern California, sometimes occurs inland.

40a (38) Plants with at least some plants with broad, floating blades, round oval or broadly elliptic more than 2 cm wide, on long, slender petioles, or on stems which arise from subterranean rootstocks, the petioles (when stout) sometimes supporting blades in the air when water has receded 41

40b Plants with smaller leaves, shaped and arranged otherwise 46

41a Leaves peltate 42

41b Leaves not peltate, but with marginal petioles; blades deeply lobed basally 44

42a Floating blades linear-oblong, from a weakly erect, submersed stem that also bears opposite, finely dissected leaves (Fanwort, Parrot Feather). Fig. 33 .... *Cabomba*

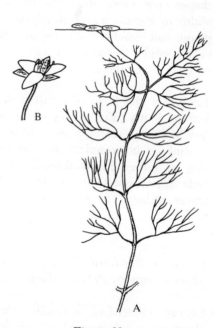

Figure 33

Figure 33 *Cabomba caroliniana* (Nymphaeaceae) A. Portion of stem showing finely dissected submersed leaves and peltate floating leaves; B. Flower.

This species has both floating blades, oblong or obovate in shape, and highly dissected submersed leaves. The small waterlily flowers are white with yellow spots. *Cabomba* is useful as an aerator and is popular as a fish aquarium plant. Thus far the species is known from eastern and southern United States.

42b **Plants without finely dissected, submersed leaves** **43**

43a **Leaves oval or elliptic, about 5 cm in long diameter, the petioles and stem thickly coated with a firm mucilage; flowers relatively small (lotuslike), sometimes opening under water (Water Shield). Fig. 34** .... ***Brasenia***

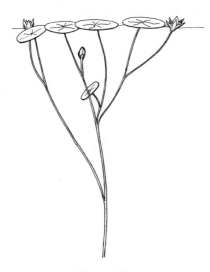

Figure 34

Figure 34 *Brasenia Schreberi* (Nymphaeaceae). Portion of plant showing leaves with peltate, floating blades.

This species is widely distributed but somewhat uncommon. The plants grow in quiet water, often among emergent reeds and rushes. The firm, mucilaginous coating on the stem and petioles is so slippery that collecting by hand is difficult.

43b **Leaves much larger, 3 dm or more across, blades often held above the water surface by a stout petiole; flowers light yellow, large, showy, lotuslike blooms (Lotus). Fig. 35** .... ***Nelumbo***

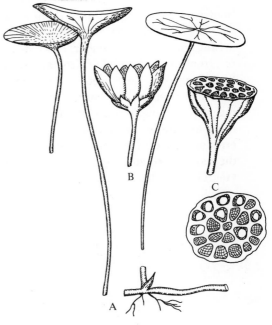

Figure 35

Figure 35 *Nelumbo lutea* (Nymphaeaceae) A. Rhizome and portions of emergent, peltate leaves; B. Lotus type of blossom; C. Receptacle with nutlike fruits (Chinquapins).

The American Lotus occurs mostly throughout the Ohio and lower Mississippi valleys, although in favorable situations it grows in upper Midwest and New England states. It has been reported also from eastern Texas and Oklahoma as well as from Virginia. The lotus forms dense meadows in lakes and lagoons, with the peltate leaves usually raised above the water surface on stout petioles. The disc-like receptacle has "pepperbox" sockets in which nutlike fruits develop. These are known as Chinquapins and are collected for food by both Man and animals. A tribe of Indians in the South were known as the Chinquapin Eaters. The rhizome is also used as food by muskrats.

44a (41) Leaves with orbicular or cordate blades, with crenate margins, floating at the surface on long, slender petioles arising from either a slender, erect stem, or from a horizontal rhizome, veins branching and then recurved to unite with one another; the upright stem giving rise to aquatic roots at the base of the leaf petiole; flowers solitary or several together arising from the erect stem, the corolla rotate, 5-parted (Floating Heart). Fig. 36 .... *Nymphoides*

which are clustered at the end of horizontal rhizomes. The rhizomes usually have runners. Flower stalks and adventitious roots develop from the upper section of the petioles. There are several species, all known from eastern and southern United States. *Nymphoides* is a useful acquarium plant.

44b Plants otherwise **45**

45a Leaves broadly oval (up to 2 times the width in length), or nearly round, with broadly rounded basal lobes which (often) overlap, the margins entire; flowers yellow, tuliplike; fruit a swollen, flat-topped urn with a broad stigmatic surface (Yellow Water Lily). Fig. 37 .... ***Nuphar***

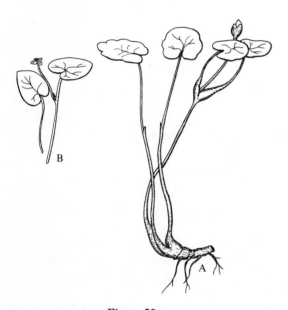

Figure 36

Figure 36 *Nymphoides* (Menyanthaceae). A. *Nymphoides peltatum;* B. Leaves and flower of *N. cordatum.*

The deeply lobed blades have a palmate venation and float at the surface on long petioles

Figure 37

Figure 37 *Nuphar* (Nymphaeaceae) A, B. Leaf and flower of *N. advena;* C. Leaf of *N. variegatum;* D. Rhizome.

This genus has yellow, tuliplike flowers and broadly oval, bilobed leaf blades on long petioles that grow from thick, subterranean rhizomes. Petioles may be as much as 12 feet long. Young, submersed leaves are often red-tinged. The lobes of the leaf often overlap, especially in *N. advena*. This is perhaps the most widely distributed species throughout eastern United States; others are somewhat local in several sections of the country. *N. poly-sepalum* occurs in the west and northwest. Many birds and animals make use of the flowers, seeds, leaves and rhizomes, the latter being the chief source of food for muskrats. Deer and moose browse on the leaves, as do insects.

45b   **Leaves nearly round in outline, with lobes which have a prominent recurved apiculation; flowers white (or violet; cultivated species variously colored), lotuslike; fruit a globular, fleshy body with a narrow, median, stigmatic surface (Water Lily). Fig. 38 .... *Nymphaea***

Figure 38

Figure 38   *Nymphaea*   (Nymphaeaceae) Leaves and blossom.

This genus has relatively large, showy, lotus-like blooms, white or violet. The leaf blades are nearly circular but are deeply lobed. At the base of each lobe is a recurved apiculation. One common species, *N. odorata* is purple on the underside of the leaves and has purple stripes on the petioles, *N. tetragona* has

flowers one-fourth the size of the more common *N. odorata* and *N. tuberosa*. *N. tetragona* has a curious disjunct distribution throughout the United States, occurring in the northeast and northwest sections, with one station known from the Great Lakes region. *Nymphaea* occurs along with *Nuphar* but may be more common by itself in soft or acid-water habitats.

46a   **(40) Leaves simple (sometimes occurring on plants which have compound leaves also as in some species of *Rorippa*, Fig. 72), or simple at first and becoming compound, (the fern *Ceratopteris*, Fig. 87, *e.g.*). 47**

46b   **Leaves compound, sometimes finely dissected to form filiform, threadlike divisions 180**

47a   **Plants with whorled leaves, (one of which may be finely dissected) or more than 2 arising from one node (sometimes with alternate leaves also 48**

47b   **Leaves opposite, alternate or basal 58**

48a   **Plant consisting of a short, floating stem with broadly oval, dorsal leaves and finely dissected ventral leaves which are submersed (see choice No. 21a) (Water Fern; Floating Moss). Fig. 20 .... *Salvinia***

48b   **Plants otherwise 49**

49a   **Stems semi-woody, spongy at the base, perennial rootstocks giving rise to deciduous, slender, bent and whiplike and sometimes trailing branches; (leaves** commonly opposite as well as whorled on the same stem) (Swamp Loosestrife). Fig. 24 .... *Decodon*

49b Plants with definitely herbaceous stems, without branches as above **50**

50a Plants lax and buoyed in open water; sometimes rooted at first and then becoming unattached and drifting freely **51**

50b Plants definitely rooted, not drifting or buoyed in the water; growing erect, emergent or submersed; or prostrate **54**

51a Plants with oblong, floating, peltate blades; only lower leaves finely dissected and whorled (Fanwort; Parrot Feather). Fig. 33 .... *Cabomba*

51b Plants with differently shaped leaves **52**

52a Leaves with deltoid blades on long petioles which are inflated, alternate but forming a whorled rosette at the surface (Water Chestnut). Fig. 39 .... *Trapa*

Figure 39

Figure 39 *Trapa natans* (Onagraceae) A. Habit of plant with upper leaves forming a rosette, lateral leaves with inflated petiole, highly branched adventitious roots; B. Fruit.

The stem of this plant is long and lax; bears deltoid leaves which have an inflated petiole. In the lower part of the stem are numerous, finely branched adventitious roots which increase gas absorption. The subterranean roots show a negative phototropism and emerge into the water, further increasing the gas-absorbing surfaces. The solitary flowers have a two-chambered ovary in which large, triangular seeds are produced. The fleshy seed (Water Chestnut) is used for food, especially in Chinese dishes. This species, introduced from Asia, is known from eastern and northeastern United States, especially in habitats with organic mud bottoms.

52b Leaves shaped otherwise **53**

53a Leaves narrowly ovoid, or elliptic (in one species nearly linear), 3 (rarely more) at each node (rarely 2 opposite leaves); plants dioecious; pistillate flowers floating at the surface on thread-like stalks, petals 3, white or pink (Waterweed). Fig. 40 .... *Elodea*

Figure 40 *Elodea* (Hydrocharitaceae) A. *E. densa,* portion of stem; B. *E. canadensis* with carpellate flower; C. Carpellate flower enlarged; D. *E. occidentalis,* portion of stem bearing narrow, nearly linear leaves; E. *Hydrilla verticillata* leaf; F. *E. canadensis* leaf stylized.

Anacharis is a synonym for this genus known commonly as Water Weed. The stems are bushy with whorls of ovate leaves. The plants reproduce actively by fragmentation and although they develop as rooted stems they frequently become free-floating. The two most common and dioecious species in this country are *E. canadensis* and *E. occidentale.* The latter has slender, nearly linear leaves, the former ovate, either lax or sometimes rigid. Not infrequently *E. canadensis* becomes coated with lime.

Elodea densa, introduced from Brazil might be considered an 'escape' but it is now well-established in local areas. This species forms profuse, often troublesome growths especially in Pacific coast states.

All species are popular as aquarium plants because they are efficient oxygenators and are aesthetic. Carpellate flowers are white or pinkish, borne on long, threadlike peduncles that arise from a basal, submersed spathe. The flowers float at the surface in such a way as to expose the curved styles and stigmatic organs. The staminate flowers occur in a basal spathe, are released so that they float about on the water surface where they come in contact with the carpellate flowers.

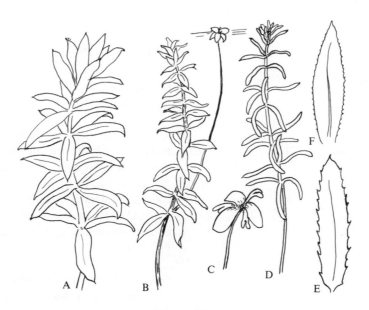

Figure 40

Hydrilla verticillata is very similar to *Elodea* species and collections of the latter, especially *E. densa* should be compared with it. *Hydrilla* is a tropical and mostly African genus that has been introduced to England and to parts of the United States. It is differentiated from *Elodea* in the vegetative condition (Fig. 40E) by having leaves with sinuate-crenate margins, each crena tipped with a spiny projection. *Elodea* has entire leaf margins, not sinuate, but has many, closely arranged teeth (one-celled). Leaves of *Hydrilla* occur in whorls of 5; *Elodea canadensis* with leaves in 3's.

53b Leaves narrowly linear, many at each node (rarely with some leaves alternate on the same stem also) (Water Mare's Tail). Fig. 41 .... *Hippuris*

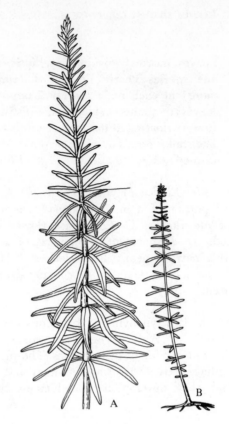

Figure 41

Figure 41 *Hippuris vulgaris* (Haloragidaceae) A. Habit of plant with submersed and emergent stem and leaves; B. Habit of marginal plant with somewhat rigid leaves.

These plants are limp and flexible when submersed, with whorls of lax leaves, but are erect and rigid, with short leaves when emergent. It is highly useful as an oxygenator. The species is widely distributed throughout the United States and occurs as one of the few aquatic plants in arctic pools and lakes.

54a (50) Plants sprawling, either on the shore or in shallow water 55

54b Plants erect, usually conspicuously emergent or growing along shores **56**

55a Leaves deeply lobed (simple but nearly compound), 3 at a node (although usually opposite) teeth bluntly pointed; flowers green, solitary in the axils of leaves. Fig. 42 ....

.... *Leucospora* (*Conobea*)

This is the only species in the genus; grows on shores or in lake marginal water. It is found mostly in midwestern United States, but occurs southward. The leaves are either opposite or whorled and are deeply pinnate-lobed. The greenish flowers are borne singly (usually) in the axils of leaves. There is no known biological importance.

55b Leaves simple, linear or oblong, entire margins, several (usually 4) in a whorl at each node; flowers small (2-3 mm wide), white, stalked, in a cyme borne in the axils of leaf whorls; stems 4-angled (Bedstraw). Fig. 43 .... *Galium*

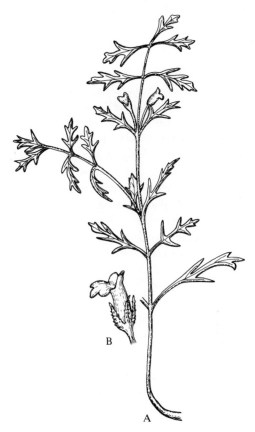

Figure 42

Figure 42 *Leucospora multifida* (*Conobea*) (Scrophulariaceae) A. Habit of plant with opposite, deeply incised leaves; B. Single flower.

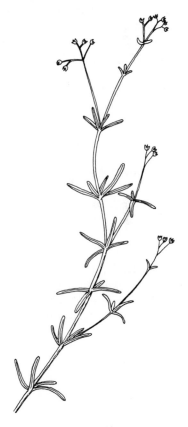

Figure 43

Figure 43 *Galium* (Rubiaceae) A. Portion of branch of *Galium tinctorium.*

In this genus there are whorls of linear leaves and panicles of small, white flowers (or sometimes only one, or two). Submersed species are not beset with hooklike spines as are the terrestrial ones. *G. trifidum* has thin, hooked, flower stalks whereas in *G. tinctorium* they are thicker and straight.

56a (54) **Erect stems with many elongate and linear leaves (6-12) at each node (a bottle-brush type of growth); upper leaves short and somewhat rigid (2-3 mm wide), lower leaves (especially if submersed) long and lax, collapsing when removed from the water (Water Mare's Tail). Fig. 41** .... *Hippuris*

56b Erect stem with leaves shaped and arranged otherwise 57

57a Short herbs, about 1/2 M, with rounded, oval or mostly lanceolate leaves, opposite or alternate (See 58b), but sometimes whorled; leaves gland-dotted and often with a fringe along the basal margin of the very short petiole; base of leaf tapering; flowers yellow (often purple-spotted), either solitary in the axils of leaves or in a terminal raceme, capsule of flower globular; ovary and capsule 1-celled (Loosestrife). Fig. 44 .... *Lysimachia*

Figure 44 *Lysimachia* (Primulaceae) A. *Lysimachia thyrsiflora;* B. *L. ciliata.*

This genus shows considerable variation in leaf arrangement, but usually they have glandular dots and most species have ciliate fringes along the basal margins of the blade as well as along the petioles. The latter character varies in different parts of the United States. *L. terrestris* with square stems and *L. thyrsiflora* with round stems are the most common species. The latter occurs both in the water (emergent) and along lake shores, in wet meadows, etc.

57b **Tall, often rank herbs, as much as 2 M high; leaves ovate to linear-lanceolate, and sessile, sometimes whorled but mostly opposite (see 58b), usually somewhat heart-shaped or lobed at the base which is not fringed along the margins, sessile on usually somewhat angular stems; flowers purple (or white), in long terminal spikes (or in some species solitary in the axils of leaves); capsule subcylindric; ovary and capsule 2-celled (Spiked Loosestrife). Fig. 45** ....
.... *Lythrum*

Figure 44

Figure 45

Figure 45 *Lythrum salicaria* (Lythraceae)
A. Portion of stem bearing axillary flowers;
B. Single flower.

This is a tall, rank weed, growing along shores
and in wet meadows. The purple flowers are
in terminal spikes. The leaves are sessile, with
a slightly lobed base. *L. salicaria* and *L. ala-
tum* are two species distributed throughout
eastern and southern United States. The former has the upper leaves shorter and partly
hidden by the dense flowers.

58a (47) Leaves opposite (But see *Lud-
    wigia polycarpa*, p. 47) 59

58b Leaves alternate or basal 106

59a Plants floating; leaves opposite 60

59b Plants anchored by roots, in the water
    or on shore; leaves opposite 61

60a Plant consisting of a pair of opposite,
    leaflike segments or joints, about 5 to 8
    mm wide, the under side purple and
    bearing several rootlets from each joint
    (Great Duckweed). Fig. 3 .... *Spirodela*

60b Plant a short, floating stem with 2 or 3
    pairs of opposite, circular leaves, 1 cm
    or less across, bearing stiff bristles on
    the upper surface; no roots but highly
    divided ventral leaves (Floating Fern).
    Fig. 20 .... *Salvinia*

61a Leaves with entire margins 62

61b Leaves with teeth, serrations, or crenu-
    late, or margin lobed and incised 89

62a Plants submersed and essentially rooted
    to the bottom, sometimes at 5 M (often
    becoming free-floating); with or with-
    out floating leaves 63

62b Plants rooted on shore or in shallow
    water, emergent, sprawling or growing
    erect at margins of aquatic habitats ......
    70

63a Plants with variously shaped leaves:
    linear lanceolate, elliptic or ribbonlike,
    sometimes with oval floating leaves;
    leaves mostly alternate, but rarely oppo-
    site, with a stipule at the base of the
    leaf, free or forming a sheath about the
    stem just above the leaf attachment
    (Pondweed). Fig. 46 .... *Potamogeton*

Figure 46

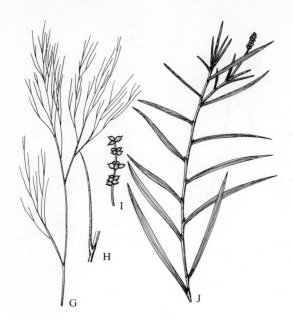

Figure 46 Continued

Figure 46 Continued

Figure 46 Continued

Figure 46   *Potamogeton* (Potamogetonaceae) A. *Potamogeton natans;* B. *P. richardsonii;* C. *P. gramineus;* D. *Potamogeton* flower, side view (diagrammatic); E. Flower, vertical view (diagrammatic); F. *P. natans* fruit; G. *P. pectinatus;* H. *P. pectinatus,* leaf and stipule; I. *P. pectinatus* fruits; J. *P. robbinsii;* K. *P. amplifolius;* L. *P. zosteriformis;* M. *P. praelongus,* habit of a portion of stem and showing keel-shaped leaf tip which splits when pressed.

This is the Pondweed genus, with about 45 species distributed in the United States. The leaves are variable in shape; broad blades, ribbons, or narrowly linear. Some have both narrow, submersed leaves and broad, floating (oval or elliptic) blades. The alternate leaves with a stipule, and the morphology of the flowers and fruits are characteristic features which separate this genus from other aquatics. The flowers have a perianth composed of a 4-lobed calyx, 4 stamens and usually 4 carpels, each of which forms a one-seeded drupe.

Many species are highly important for bird and animal food, in oxygenation of water, and because of the substantial amount of organic matter they produce in the aquatic environment.

63b Plants having leaves without stipules; leaves shaped differently 64

64a Stem bushy with opposite (but mostly whorled), elliptic or oval, sessile leaves, arranged along the entire length; small white (5-8 mm) carpellate flowers floating at the surface on long, white threads from the submersed stem; staminate flowers with 3 sepals and petals, bearing 3-9 anthers, borne sessile in the axils of leaves and submersed (Waterweed). Fig. 40 .... *Elodea*

64b Stems with leaves shaped and arranged otherwise 65

65a Plants with a pair of oval, floating leaf blades and highly dissected, submersed leaves (Fanwort, Parrot Feather). Fig. 33 .... *Cabomba*

65b Plants with leaves shaped and arranged otherwise 66

66a Plants with slender, mostly vertical, threadlike stems bearing narrow, elongate or spatula-shaped opposite leaves which are crowded and form a rosette at the surface (at least when fully developed); flower solitary, sessile in axils of leaves; fruit bilobed, nutlike (Water Starwort). Fig. 47 .... *Callitriche*

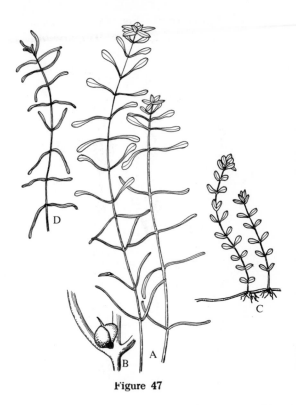

Figure 47

Figure 47 *Callitriche* (Callitrichaceae) A. *Callitriche palustris*, habit; B. Fruit; C. *C. deflexa* habit; D. *C. hermaphroditica* habit.

This genus is characterized by the slender, threadlike submersed stems which often do not reach the surface. Leaves are linear to spatula-shaped on the same plant and they may become crowded and form a rosette at the water surface, hence the name Water Starwort. The tender plants are used by diving birds for food.

66b Plants with leaves shaped and arranged otherwise 67

67a Plants growing erect or essentially so, or lax, especially in submersed species, with oval, elliptic to lanceolate leaves which are sessile; leaves with translucent dots when emergent (Goat Weed;

St. John's-wort). Fig. 48 ....
.... *Hypericum*(*)

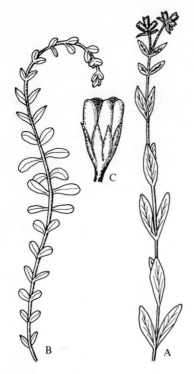

Figure 48

Figure 48 *Hypericum* (Hypericaceae) A.
Hypericum boreale; B. *H. ellipticum;* C. *H. punctatum* flower.

Several species of the genus grow either submersed or emergent, and on lake shores, wet
meadows, *etc.* The leaves are oval or lanceolate, sessile and usually have transparent spots
in the blades, especially when leaves are above
water. In most species the flowers are yellow,
in both terminal and axilary racemes or
corymbs. Several species are known to be used
for food by birds and browsing animals.

**67b Plants otherwise, creeping, sometimes
with erect shoots** **68**

68a Leaves linear or in some species oblong-
lanceolate with entire margins; plants
with creeping rootstocks from which
erect or sprawling shoots arise, forming
extensive floating mats, especially in
shallow water; flowers 5-parted, in heads
which are either axial and sessile or on
long shoots, either terminal on the stem
or in the axils of leaves; (plants also
marginal, growing on mud flats) (Alligator Weed). Fig. 49 ...... *Alternanthera*

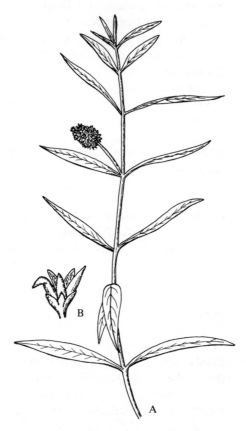

Figure 49

(*) *Hypericum virginicum* with showy pink-
purple flowers is found often in bogs and
swamps. The name is synonymous with *Tria-
denum virginicum.*

Figure 49 *Alternanthera philoxeroides* (Amaranthaceae) A. Habit of plant portion; B. Single flower.

This species is known from the Gulf region of the United States. It is a low, sprawling weed with narrowly elliptic, opposite leaves and with heads of small flowers on a long peduncle. Plants grow abundantly in ponds and slowly flowing streams.

68b Plants otherwise; leaves shaped differently 69

69a Leaves broadly oval to nearly round, sessile and somewhat clasping the stem; plants greenish; flowers in 2's and 3's in the axils of leaves; leaves palmately veined (Water Hyssop). Fig. 50 ....
.... *Bacopa* (*Hydrotrida*)

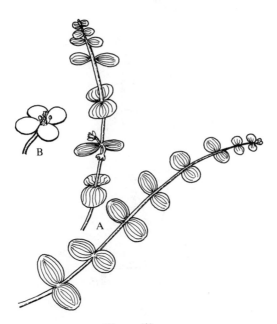

Figure 50

Figure 50 *Bacopa* (*Bramia*) (Scrophulariaceae) A. Branches with nearly circular leaves and axial flowers; B. Single flower.

In this genus plants are sprawling or creeping and bushy. The small, yellow, two-lipped flowers are solitary in the axils of leaves. The common species is *Bacopa monnieria*, a plant of shores and of brackish ponds on the Atlantic and Gulf coasts.

69b Leaves elliptic or oval, mostly tapering at the base and usually with a petiole (sessile, but with a narrowed base in some species), 1-4 cm long; leaves pinnately veined (False Loosestrife). Fig. 51 .... (See *Jussiaea* in couplet 135a) *Ludwigia*

Figure 51 *Ludwigia* (Onagraceae) A. *Ludwigia polycarpa*; B. *L. palustris*; C. Calyx; D. *L. linearis*; E. Fruit.

There are many species of *Ludwigia*, erect and terrestrial, or prostrate and creeping on shores, or submersed. The common aquatic species is *L. palustris*, a somewhat fleshy herb with opposite leaves and with urnlike, sessile flowers in the axils. Stems and leaves are reddish. It is a species widely distributed over the United States. Plants are used by muskrats for food.

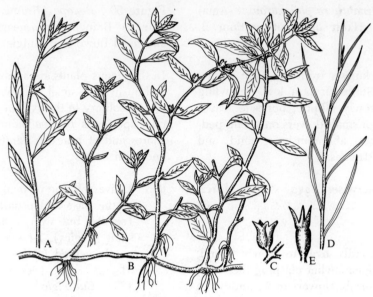

Figure 51

70a (62) Plants of dwarf stature, no more than 10 cm long or high, mostly creeping, with some erect branches 71

70b Plants larger, erect in part or completely so 72

71a Plants 6-8 cm high, with succulent, puffy, somewhat linear leaves which are joined at their bases; plants mostly of tidal marshes (Pigmy Weed). Fig. 52 .... *Tillaea*

This is a small, tufted and sprawling weed with opposite, linear and succulent leaves. It is found in brackish situations along all coasts, but apparently is known from only a few locations. It is the only member of the Crassulaceae which is aquatic or semi-aquatic.

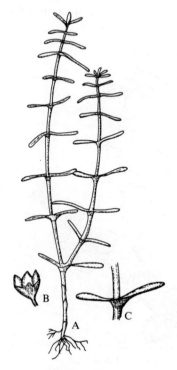

Figure 52

Figure 52 *Tillaea aquatica* (Crassulaceae) A. Habit; B. Single flower; C. Opposite leaves joined at the base.

71b Plants up to 10 cm long or high; leaves narrowly oval to nearly linear, somewhat spatulate in some species, narrowed at the base and not adjoined; plants of muddy bottoms or in tidal flats, prostrate and sometimes matted (Waterwort). Fig. 53 .... *Elatine*

Figure 53

Figure 53 *Elatine triandra* (Elatinaceae) Habit of plant.

There are many species of this genus which are aquatic or semiaquatic, the most widely distributed being *E. americana* which can be found in tidal marshes and on shores of ponds throughout the United States. The leaves vary from oval to oblanceolate; are glabrous and somewhat fleshy. It is thought that some species are used by ducks.

72a (70) Leaves elongate, linear (oblong), approaching lanceolate in some **73**

72b Leaves other shaped, mostly lanceolate or oblong lanceolate **77**

73a Leaves with transparent or translucent dots (except that they may not show in submersed leaves), seen by holding leaf to the light and examining with a hand lens (Goat Weed; St. John's-wort). Fig. 48 .... *Hypericum*

73b Leaves without transcluent dots **74**

74a Plants with hard or semi-woody stems, especially at the base; leaves bluntly pointed; flowers soitary in leaf axils; calyx cylindrical and striated (Spiked Loosestrife). Fig. 45 .... *Lythrum* (*L. lineare*)

74b Plants not tough and semi-woody at the stem base **75**

75a Leaves sharply pointed at the apex and long-tapering, about 12 mm wide; prominent lateral veins from a conspicuous midrib; flowers in sessile or stalked heads (Alligator Weed). Fig. 49 .... *Alternanthera*

75b Leaves smaller, 1.5 to 6 mm wide, shaped differently; flowers arranged otherwise **76**

76a Leaves blunt-pointed or very briefly tapering; sessile, mostly oblong or eliptic but sometimes approaching linear; calyx bell-shaped with deep, rounded lobes; plants of coastal regions or salt marshes (Sea Milkwort). Fig. 25 .... *Glaux*

76b Leaves blunt-pointed or rounded at the apex, not sessile but with short petioles, oblanceolate to spatulate; calyx urn-shaped with short-pointed lobes (Tooth-cup). Fig. 54 .... *Rotala*

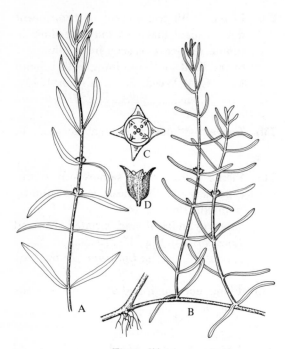

Figure 54

Figure 54 *Rotala* (Lythraceae) A. *Rotala ramosior;* B. *R. diandra;* C., D. Flower in vertical and lateral views.

Plants have erect stems which may be as much as 50 cm tall with opposite, elliptical, oval or oblanceolate leaves. The solitary flowers in the leaf axils produce urnlike, 4-valved capsules. Plants inhabit shores and wet meadows. *R. ramosior* is known from rice fields.

77a (72) Leaves lanceolate or oblong lance-olate (See Fig. 45) 78

77b Leaves other shapes 81

78a Plants erect with elongate-lanceolate, acutely pointed leaves that are dotted with dark glands; flowers yellow, in dense terminal or axial racemes, in some species the stems angular because of ridges (Loosestrife). Fig. 44 .... *Lysimachia* (*L. thyrsiflora*)

78b Leaves without dark glands; flowers arranged otherwise 79

79a Erect shoots from creeping rootstocks; flowers in heads or short spikes on long peduncles 80

79b Plants without creeping rootstocks, erect with a semi-woody base; flowers solitary or in whorls in the axils of leaves, forming a terminal spike (Spiked Loosestrife). Fig. 45 .... *Lythrum*

80a Flowers purple, the corolla irregular with the upper lip notched, the lower 3-lobed; stamens 2; leaves willowlike, rather rigid and straight, directed upward to 15 cm long; stems up to 10 dm high (Water Willow). Fig. 55 .... *Dianthera*

Figure 55

Figure 55 *Dianthera* (*Justicia*) *americana* (Acanthaceae) A. Section of stem and one axial inflorescence; B. Single flower.

This species occurs throughout eastern and midwestern states. The opposite, elongate-elliptic leaves are similar to those of a willow. The small, purple flowers are in heads on long peducles. *D. ovata* occurs mostly in southern states. The seeds of *Dianthera* are eaten by grouse.

80b Flowers greenish or white, with a peri-anth of 5 sepals unequal in length; leaves oblong-lanceolate, but often nearly linear, not rigid, curved and somewhat drooping (Alligator Weed). Fig. 49 .... *Alternanthera*

81a (77) Leaves elliptical or elongate-ellip-tic (sometimes nearly lanceolate) 82

81b Leaves broadly oval to nearly round (some species with linear or elongate leaves also on the same stem) 87

82a Plants with semi-woody, perennial bases giving rise to whiplike, annual branches (Swamp Loosestrife). Fig. 24 .... *Decodon*

82b Plants otherwise 83

83a Flowers and fruits borne in terminal racemes or in clusters, or one or two on stalks in the axils of upper leaves 84

83b Flowers and fruits solitary and sessile in the axils of leaves 85

84a Leaves, especially when emergent, show-ing translucent dots when held to the light (Goat Weed; St. John's-wort). Fig. 48 .... *Hypericum*

84b Leaves without translucent dots; often with fringes along the lower margins of leaves (Loosestrife). Fig. 44 .... *Lysimachia*

85a (83) Plants dwarf, 4-5 cm long; pros-trate on shores, portions erect when sub-mersed, but very limp; fruit a thin-walled pod, showing the seeds; leaves 1 cm long or less (Waterwort). Fig. 53 .... *Elatine*

85b Plants larger, with different type of fruit 86

86a Plants with ascending stems from a slender rootstock; leaves usually opposite below, alternate above; perianth of 5 calyx lobes (no petals), and whitish; ovary superior; fruit a beaked capsule with the style persisting (Sea Milkwort). Fig. 25 .... *Glaux*

86b Plants prostrate on and rooting in mud, with roots from stem nodes, or floating on the water; (some species erect, and if so, with linear-lanceolate leaves); leaves mostly opposite throughout the stem (in some species broadly oval to nearly round); perianth of 4, usually reddish sepals; ovary inferior; fruit a capsule, broader than long or enlarged above the middle (False Loosestrife). Fig. 51 .... *Ludwigia*

87a (81) Leaves, especially when emergent, with translucent spots, easily seen with a hand lens when the leaf is held to the light (Goat Weed; St. John's-wort). Fig. 48 .... *Hypericum*

87b Leaves without translucent spots 88

88a Sprawling and creeping plants (or with floating stems); flowers stalked, solitary in the axils of leaves (Water Hyssop). Fig. 50 .... *Bacopa*

88b Plants erect; stems not woody, but hard and stiff; flowers purple (Spiked Loosestrife). Fig. 45 .... *Lythrum*

89a (61) Leaves crenulate, sometimes with sharp crenulations approaching serrations (See Fig. 42); sometimes crenulations deep, so as to form lobes which have entire margins 90

89b Leaves with serrate margins (sometimes with coarse serrations, so deep as to give a nearly lobed condition as in *Lycopus americanus*, e.g.) 95

90a Plants with stipules at the base of the leaves (usually leaves alternate, but rarely opposite or nearly so); leaf margins with numerous, minute crenulations (Pondweed). Fig. 56 .... *Potamogeton crispus*

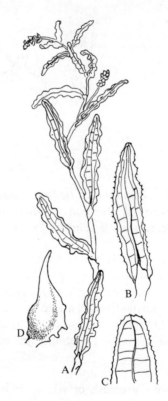

Figure 56

Figure 56 *Potamogeton crispus* (Polamoge-tonaceae) A. Portion of stem showing crinkled and undulate margins of leaves; B., C. Leaves showing venation; D. Fruit.

This is the only species of *Potamogeton* which does not have entire leaf margins. It is generally distributed throughout the United States wherever there are suitable habitats.

90b   Plants without stipules 91

91a   Leaves deeply lobed, pinnately divided and nearly compound. Fig. 42 ....
.... *Leucospora*

91b   Leaves not lobed, crenulations some-times few and nearly lacking 92

92a   Flowers numerous, relatively small, in racemes in the axils of leaves (terminal racemes also) which are sessile and in some species clasping the stem, up to 20 mm wide (Speedwell). Fig. 57 ....
.... *Veronica*

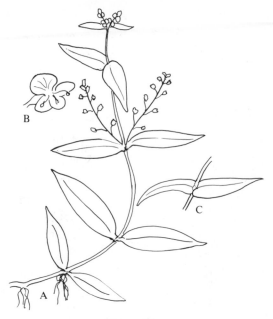

Figure 57

Figure 57   *Veronica* (Scrophulariaceae) A. *Veronica americana* habit; B. Single flower; C. Leaves.

There are several species which are semi-aquatic, the most common being *V. americana.* The elliptic or lanceolate leaves are coarsely serrate. The blue and white corollas are irregular, the flowers arranged in terminal or axial racemes. Except that beds of plants serve as good soil binders there is no known biological importance.

92b   Flowers solitary (or 2, 3) in the axils of leaves 93

93a   Leaf margins conspicuously crenulate (sometimes somewhat serrate); flowers showy, distinctly bilobed or 2-lipped, yellow, rose or blue (Monkey Flower). Fig. 58 .... *Mimulus*

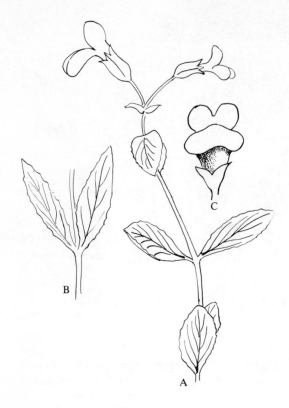

Figure 58

94a Plants low and creeping, often rooting at the nodes (frequently floating); flowers with 4 stamens, all with anthers (Water Hyssop). Fig. 50 .... *Bacopa*

94b Plants erect, to 3 cm high; flowers with 4 stamens, only 2 with anthers (False Pimpernel). Fig. 59 .... *Lindernia*

Figure 58   *Mimulus* (Scrophulariaceae) A. *Mimulas guttatus;* B. M. *alatus* leaves; C. Flower, *M. guttatus.*

This genus includes several species that inhabit pond and stream margins, or occur in springs where they often become rank and sprawling. The flowers are usually yellow, but *M. lewisii* is bright pink to rose-colored and *M. ringens* is blue. *M. moschatus* is a low creeping species bearing sticky hairs; appears woolly.

93b Leaf margins with few crenulations (or none); flowers nearly regular or weakly bilobed, sometimes campanulate **94**

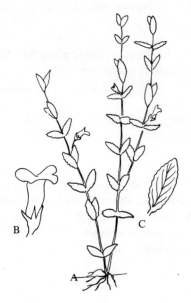

Figure 59

Figure 59   *Lindernia dubia* (Scrophulariaceae) A. Habit; B. Flower; C. Leaf.

This species and *L. anagallidea* are the most common species, growing along stream and pond margins. The opposite leaves (15 mm long) are ovate in the latter species, become distinctly smaller toward the upper section of the stem. The purple flowers are on slender, axial stalks.

95a (89) Flowers in loose racemes which are terminal on branches arising from the axils of leaves; leaves 5-20 mm wide (Speed-well). Fig. 57 .... *Veronica*

95b Flowers arranged otherwise, solitary, clustered in heads or in spikes 96

96a Flowers solitary (or 2, 3, 4), sessile in the axils of leaves 97

96b Flowers in whorls or dense clusters in the axils of leaves, forming heads, or in spikes 101

97a Plants with relatively small, succulent leaves (6 mm to 2 cm long, rarely as much as 4 cm) with wax droplets; stems hollow; flowers tubular (Hedge Hyssop). Fig. 60 .... *Gratiola*

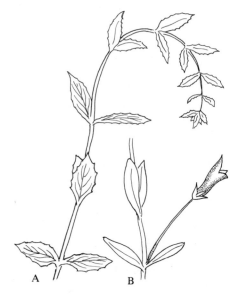

Figure 60

Figure 60 *Gratiola* (Scrophulariaceae) A. *Gratiola virginiana;* B. *G. lutea* flower.

The somewhat tubular, 2-lipped, yellow and white flowers contain stiff bristles in the throat. Some species are submersed but mostly *Gratiola* occurs on muddy shores. The plants are either annual or perennial, with somewhat succulent leaves. *G. neglecta* is common and widely distributed over the United States. There apparently is no biological importance.

97b Plants with thin leaves and mostly larger than above; stems not hollow (but some growth forms of *Mimulus* may be hollow) 98

98a Plants creeping, often rooting at the nodes; leaves often nearly entire, with few serrations 100

98b Plants erect; serrations conspicuous .. 99

99a Flowers tubular-campanulate, 2-lipped, with the upper lip strongly arched; flowers blue (Skullcap). Fig. 61 .... *Scutellaria*

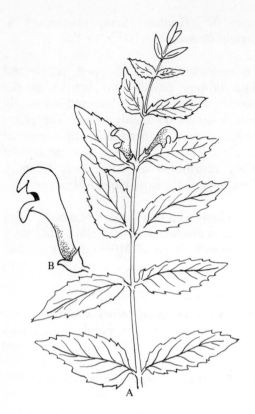

Figure 61

Figure 61 *Scutellaria epilobifolia* (Labiatae)
A. Habit; B. Flower.

This is the most common species in aquatic situations. It has showy, purple, tubular flowers which have an arched corolla. The plants grow in marshes and wet meadows and swales. The leaves are sessile, whereas in S. *laterifolia* they are petiolate with flowering shoots axial. Typical of the family, the stems are 4-angled.

99b Flowers mostly funnelform, bilobed, the upper lobe composed of one petal spreading from the funnel, the lower lip composed of 4 petals, the corolla (yellow, blue or rose) forming the familiar "monkey face" (Monkey Flower). Fig. 58 .... *Mimulus*

100a (98) Stems and leaves fleshy; leaves sometimes entire rather than serrate, broadly oval to nearly round; corolla extended but slightly beyond the calyx; petals white with the tube yellow (Water Hyssop). Fig. 50 ....
...... *Bacopa* (*Hydrotrida, Macuillamia*)

100b Stems and leaves not fleshy but the stem often succulent and hollow; corolla yellow, rose or purple, the throat spotted (Monkey Flower). Fig. 58 ...... *Mimulus*

101a (96) Flowers in spikes, occurring in pairs which are more and more closely arranged toward the apex; leaves usually elliptic or lanceolate (False Dragonhead). Fig. 62 .... *Physostegia*

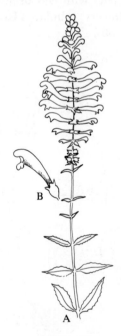

Figure 62

Figure 62 *Physostegia virginiana* (Labiatae) A. Anterior section of flowering stem; B. Single flower.

This is a tall herb with a terminal spike of showy purple or blue flowers (sometimes white). Plants inhabit weedy or grassy lake margins and swales. *P. virginiana* is perhaps the most common species and attains a height of 1½ M.

101b Flowers arranged otherwise **102**

102a Flowers arranged on a flat receptacle and usually of two forms, central ones tubular, the marginal flowers forming petal-like rays (sunflower or daisy type); emergent leaves elliptic with serrate margins; submersed leaves finely dissected (Water Marigold). Fig. 63 .... *Megalodonta*

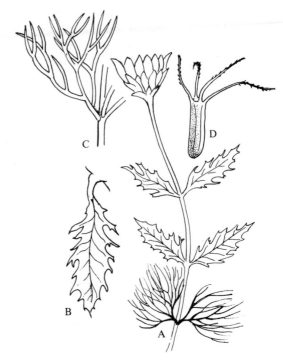

Figure 63

Figure 63 *Megalodonta beckii* (Compositae) A. Upper portion of stem showing two forms of leaves; B. Emergent leaf; C. Submersed leaf; D. Achene.

Until these submersed plants become emergent and develop their elliptical, serrate leaves, they may be confused with some species of *Ranunculus* or *Neobeckia*. The submersed leaves are finely divided dichotomously. The plants grow in relatively shallow water with silted bottoms *M. beckii*, sometimes named *Bidens beckii,* is common in northeast and northwest United States. The "daisy" type of bloom is large and conspicuous, appears above the surface of the water.

102b Flowers arranged in other types of heads, or in spikelike racemes **103**

103a Flowers closely arranged in oval or conical heads, borne on relatively long peduncles from the leaf axils; leaves with rough white hairs on the underside (Frog-fruit). Fig. 64 .... *Lippia*

Figure 64

Figure 64 *Lippia nodiflora* (Verbenaceae) Habit of plant.

Except for *Verbena* this is the only genus of the family which is semi-aquatic. The flowers are tubular, but almost rotate, with corolla slightly 2-lipped, pink or white. Plants are low and creeping and form mats on moist shores. *L. lanceolata* is the most widely distributed species whereas *L. nodiflora* seems to be confined to southern states.

103b Flowers in clusters, appearing sessile in the axils of leaves 104

104a Flowers decidedly 2-lipped, relatively large (1 cm or more long); lobes of the corolla equalling the tube in length; leaves oblong-lanceolate to elliptic (Hedge Nettle). Fig. 65 .... *Stachys*

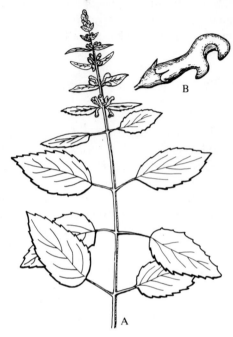

Figure 65

Figure 65 *Stachys tenuifolia* (Labiatae) A. Upper portion of stem; B. Flower.

This genus has opposite, elliptical blades with either short or long petioles. The clustered, whorled, purple flowers are tubular and 2-lipped. Species are widely distributed in marshes and along lake shores. *S. homotricha* with hairy, 4-angled stems and leaves is well-known in the eastern and midwest states.

104b Flowers relatively small, not strongly 2-lipped but almost regular 105

105a Plants aromatic (mint odor); leaves ovate to elliptic with serrations that are mostly fine, 9 to 13 or more on a side (Mint). Fig. 66 .... *Mentha*

105b Plants not aromatic; leaves oval or broadly elliptic with mostly coarse and relatively few serrations (5 to 7 on a side) (Water Horehound). Fig. 67 ....
.... *Lycopus*

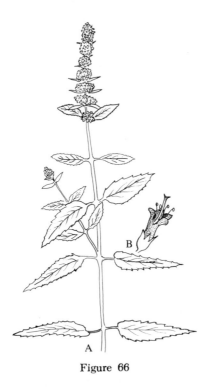

Figure 66

Figure 66 *Mentha piperata* (Labiatae) A. Upper portion of plant; B. Flower.

The species of this genus are quickly identified by their mint odor. Several are marginal or grow in moist meadows. *M. arvensis* with its dense whorls of sessile flowers is probably the most common and widely distributed. *M. spicata* with flowers in terminal spikes and without leaves in the inflorescence is spearmint. *M. piperata* with relatively large leaves is the common peppermint.

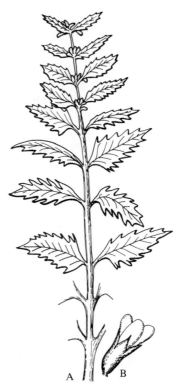

Figure 67

Figure 67 *Lycopus americana* (Labiatae) A. Anterior portion of stem; B. Single flower.

Species of this genus are mostly unbranched; have opposite, serrate or deeply lobed leaves. The flowers are in dense whorls somewhat similar to *Mentha* and other members of the family. The stem is square and often hairy. *L. americana* is probably the best-known and widely distributed, a species that is nearly glabrous. Plants are marginal or emergent in shallow water.

106a (58) Leaves alternate or in whorls of three **107**

106b Leaves basal, or in a rosette **152**

107a Plants floating, consisting of a short stem bearing pairs of broad, rounded, dorsal leaves and finely dissected submersed, ventral leaves, arranged in whorls; dorsal leaves 1/2 to 1 cm wide, bearing erect bristles on the upper epidermis (Water Fern; Floating Moss). Fig 20 .... *Salvinia*

107b Leaves shaped and arranged otherwise; plants attached or only incidentally afloat **108**

108a Leaves lobed, sometimes deeply incised or pinnately compound **109**

108b Leaves not lobed, margins serrate or entire **122**

109a Leaves broadly rounded, heart-shaped, or oval, mostly with lobed bases **110**

109b Leaves not broadly rounded but elliptic, lanceolate or other shaped **115**

110a Broad blades on long, slender petioles from submersed rootstocks; leaves floating on the surface or submersed **111**

110b Plants otherwise; blades not on long, slender petioles from submersed rootstocks **113**

111a Leaves circular in outline, reniform (peltate in some species), crenate margins

and lobed, especially at the basal attachment to the petiole; flowers small, in simple or compound umbels on a long flower stalk arising from the base of a leaf petiole (Water Pennywort). Fig. 68 .... *Hydrocotyle*

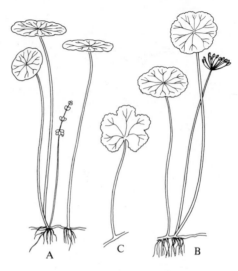

Figure 68

Figure 68 *Hydrocotyle* (Umbelliferae) A. *H. verticillata;* B. *H. umbellata;* C. *H. americana* leaf.

The round crenate leaves with long petioles are characteristic. In some species (*H. americana, H. rannunculoides*) the leaves are circular in outline but are lobed and may have a deep sinus at the point of attachment of blade and petiole. Plants are both aquatic and marginal; often are found as weeds in lawns. Some have peltate leaves. Although belonging to the wild carrot family which has flowers in umbels, some species have an inflorescence with blossoms in small heads that are sessile at the end of a long stalk.

111b Leaves circular or broadly oval with entire margins, deeply lobed at the base, mature leaf blades up to 2 dm wide 112

112a Basal lobes of leaves broadly rounded, the lobes frequently overlapping; flowers yellow, tuliplike (Yellow Water Lily). Fig. 37 .... *Nuphar*

112b Basal lobes of leaves rounded but with a short recurved apiculation; lobes usually not overlapping but spreading (Water Lily). Fig. 38 .... *Nymphaea*

113a (110) Plants with leaves distinctly heart-shaped, with the central vein prominent and the lateral veins curving to the margins in a subparallel fashion; leaves alternate, appearing to be basal; flowers small, in a spadix, enclosed by a white spathe; plants of marshes (Water Arum). Fig. 69 .... *Calla*

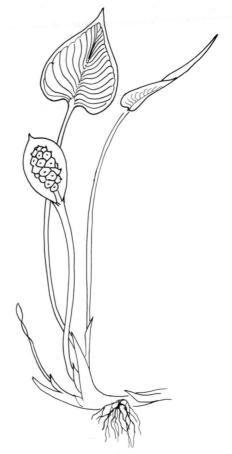

Figure 69

Figure 69 *Calla palustris* (Araceae) Habit of plant.

This is the wild Calla Lily. The involucre or spathe is white. The leaves are distinctly heart-shaped and arise in tufts from the end of a creeping rhizome. Plants may be in shallow water or in wooded swamps and are widely distributed across northern United States. The rhizome is used by muskrats for food.

113b Plants with leaves shaped otherwise and with different flowers 114

114a Leaves rhomboid or nearly circular, with serrate margins, arising either from rootstocks (basal) or from an erect stem; flowers with yellow, petallike sepals (true petals lacking), a buttercup type of bloom; plants of marshes (some species aquatic) (Marsh Marigold). Fig. 70 .... *Caltha*

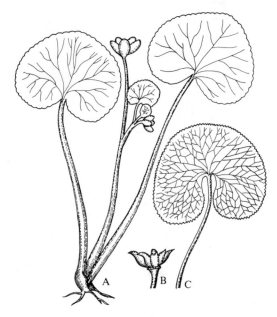

Figure 70

Figure 70 *Caltha palustris* (Ranunculaceae) A. Habit of plant; B. Follicles; C. Another leaf shape.

The flowers in this genus are relatively large and waxy, yellow (or white) sepals (no petals). Included here is the familiar Marsh Marigold, each plant growing as a dense clump of large leaves. *C. natans* is aquatic with the stems floating; occurs mostly in northern lakes. *C. palustris* and its varieties is widely distributed; appears in reduced form in the Subarctic.

114b Leaves variable, either pinnately compound with linear segments, *or* rhomboid-reniform; marginal lobes deep or shallow, often with lobings variable in form on the same plant (Buttercup). Fig. 71 .... *Ranunculus*

Figure 71 *Ranunculus* (Ranunculaceae) A. *R. flabellaris*, portion of stem; B. *R. purshii* showing two leaf forms; C. *R. aquatilis;* D. *R. ambigens;* E. *R. laxicaulis* leaf; F. *R. repens* leaves; G. *R. reptans*, a creeping species with linear leaves; H. *R. reptans* var. *ovalis.*

Species of *Ranunculus* are extremely variable in their leaf shapes and in the degree of lobings and divisions. Even the same plant may show different types of leaves. The completely submersed species have finely dissected leaves which are either limp or somewhat rigid. The buttercup flowers are either white or yellow, and may open under water. Plant stems are conspicuously light (whitish) when seen under water. Many *Ranunculus* species are used by moose and aquatic birds for food.

Figure 71

115a (109) Flowers with 4 petals, and 4 sepals (which often are deciduous), and 6 stamens; fruit a silique 116

115b Flowers different; fruit not a silique ....
.... 119

116a Flowers greenish-white, small and somewhat inconspicuous; upper leaves simple but variously crenate or coarsely toothed, lower leaves pinnately lobed, often deeply so, or pinnately compound; (leaves sometimes alternate also) (Cress). Fig. 72 .... *Rorippa*

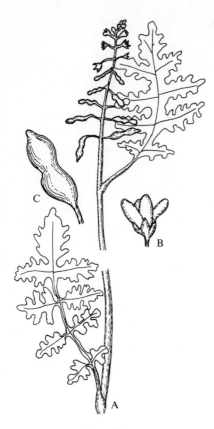

Figure 72

Figure 72 *Rorippa palustris* Var. (Cruciferae)
A. Portion of plant with terminal raceme; B. Flower; C. Fruit.

Plants in this genus have small, greenish-yellow flowers. Most are marginal; some grow emergent and erect, but *R. sylvestris* is prostrate. *R. palustris* is probably the most widely distributed species in eastern United States but *R. aquatica* (with whitish flowers) is also common. None of the species seems to have any biological importances.

116b Flowers white, yellow or lavender .. 117

117a Upper leaves simple, elongate-elliptic, either finely or coarsely serrate, the lower leaves finely dissected and pinnately compound, forming lateral tufts which break away from the stem easily; flowers in a raceme, with fruits below and buds at the apex; fruit an oval capsule-silique which has but one chamber (Lake Cress). Fig. 73 .... *Neobeckia*

Figure 73

Figure 73 *Neobeckia aquatica* (Cruciferae)
A. Habit showing finely dissected submersed leaves; B., C. Submersed and emergent leaves.

This species often appears in a vegetative condition and does not show typical mustard family flower characters. When submersed the leaves are finely dissected. *Neobeckia* often becomes a weed and crowds out other more desirable or useful aquatic plants. Immature plants should be compared with young plants of *Megalodonta*. *Neobeckia* occurs in lagoons and along slowly flowing river shores.

117b Plants without lower leaves finely dissected **118**

118a Plants mostly erect (one species sprawling and rooted at nodes) but with unbranched stems; flowers relatively large (3 to 6 mm across), white or lavender; fruit an elongate slender, podlike silique which is flattened in cross section; plants with a basal leaf different in shape from the stem leaves (Bitter Cress). Fig. 74 .... *Cardamine*

Figure 74

Figure 74 *Cardamine pratensis* Var. (Cruciferae) A. Habit of plant; B. Flower; C. Fruit.

Species of this genus are erect and little or not at all branched. Different species have characteristic and variable leaves, even on the same plant. There is a single, separate basal leaf which is always different in shape from those on the stem. Lower leaves are mostly pinnately lobed; the upper simple. Flowers are white or pink; the fruit a long, slender silique. Plants are sparsely scattered in a habitat; no biological importance is known.

118b Plants prostrate and sprawling, or semi-erect, often rank with hollow stems, much-branched; flowers small and several closely arranged in a compact panicle; fruit an elongate pod, round in cross section (Water Cress). Figure 75 .... *Nasturtium**

(*) Some botanists regard *N. officinalis* as synonymous with *Rorippa nasturtium-aquaticum.*

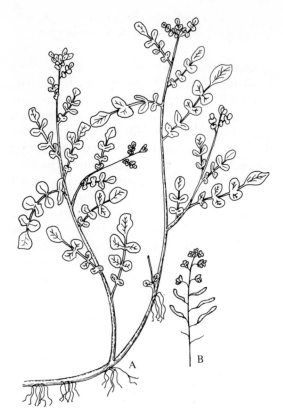

Figure 75

Figure 75 *Nasturtium officinale* (Cruciferae)
A. Habit; B. Raceme.

This is the well-known Water Cress, used as a salad. The plants are sprawling and erect, usually in spring water and may be rank and hollow-stemmed. They often root from the stem nodes. There are several varieties and forms that are recognized and differentiated according to leaf form and size.

119a (115) Flowers yellow, with 5 petals and 5 sepals; pistils numerous; leaves oval or elliptic with serrate margins; plants often with palmately lobed leaves (Buttercup). Fig. 71 .... *Ranunculus*

119b Flowers some other color, or colorless ..
.. 120

120a Flowers conspicuous, violet or purple; leaves cordate, on stems which also bear lobed leaves (Nightshade). Fig. 76
.. *Solanum*

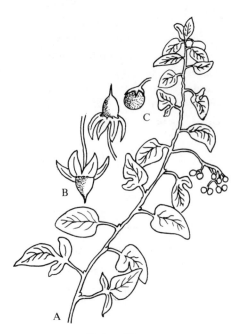

Figure 76

Figure 76 *Solanum Dulcamara* (Solanaceae)
A. Branch; B. Flowers; C. Fruit.

This plant is known as Nightshade or Bittersweet. The plants are sprawlng and vinelike, often drooping over banks and growing in the water. Leaves are simple and heart-shaped or with one or twc lobes, all on the same plant. The purple flowers produce clusters of red berries which are used by some birds.

120b Flowers other colors, or colorless 121

121a Flowers small, greenish or colorless, solitary in axils of leaves, with 3 calyx lobes but no petals; stamens 3; submersed leaves deeply incised (nearly compound), emergent leaves not lobed, but toothed along the margin (Mermaid Weed). Fig. 77 .... *Prosperinaca*

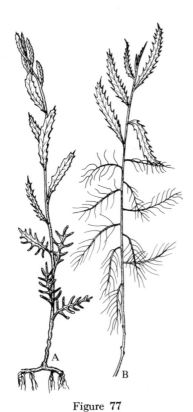

Figure 77

Figure 77 *Prosperinaca* (Haloragaceae) A. *Prosperinaca* sp. habit; B. *P. palustris*, habit showing finely dissected leaves.

There are at least three species which are aquatic or semi-aquatic. The most common and widely distributed is *P. palustris* and its varieties. The variety *amblyogona* has coarsely serrate upper leaves and deeply lobed lower leaves, especially when submersed. Some spe-

cies are known to be used by birds and muskrats.

121b Flowers small, whitish, in heads which are arranged in umbels; leaves narrowly elongate, leathery, with coarse teeth or spiniferous margins; petioles hollow; fruit ovoid with ribs and oil tubes (Eryngo; Button Snakeroot). Fig. 78 .... *Eryngium*

Figure 78

Figure 78 *Eryngium* (Umbelliferae) A. Portion of plant; B. Leaf.

Species in this genus are marginal or only incidentally growing in water. Conical heads of flowers are arranged in compound umbels. One species, *E. prostratum* is procumbent; others are erect with spiny leaves.

122a (108) Leaf margins entire 123

122b Leaf margins serrate (or sharply crenate) 143

123a Plants with a stipule or a stipular sheath
at the base of the leaf, or covering each
node, the sheath sometimes with a flar-
ing collar 124

123b Plants otherwise; without a sheath at
each node 126

124a Leaves with a prominent midvein, and
with lateral veins pinnately branching;
stipular sheath on each node; plants
sprawling or erect 125

124b Leaves parallel-veined; stipule thin and
attached to the leaf base, or forming a
close sheath about the stem; leaves variously shaped, filiform, elliptic or
broadly oval when submersed, with
elliptic or oval floating leaves in some
species (Pondweed). Fig. 46 ....
.... *Potamogeton*

125a Flowers in whorls in axils of leaves; sepals 6; leaves usualy toothed (but entire in *Rumex verticillatus*); plants erect
(Dock) Fig. 79 .... *Rumex*

Figure 79

Figure 79 *Rumex verticillatus* (Polygonaceae) A. Habit; B. Leaf; C. Fruit.

Species of this genus are mostly marginal and
are found in marshes and swamps; one occurs
in tidal flats. *R. verticillatus* is commonly seen
emergent in shallow water. Typical of the
Polygonaceae there are stem sheaths at the
base of the leaf petioles. The seeds are borne
in rather dense terminal spikes and are much
used by waterfowl.

125b Flowers in spikes; leaves entire; sepals
4 or 5; aquatic species sprawling, terrestrial species erect (Smartweed). Fig. 80
.... *Polygonum*

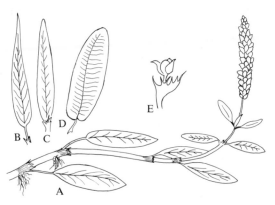

Figure 80

Figure 80 *Polygonum* (Polygonaceae) A. *Polygonum natans;* B. *P. setaceum* leaf; C. *P. hydropiperoides* leaf; D. *P. coccineum* fa. *natans* leaf; E. Single flower and sheath.

Species of this genus may be entirely aquatic, marginal, or amphibious. The plants are so well-adapted to both an aquatic and a terrestrial existence that the same plant may have portions under water and some branches erect on land. Aquatic species have foating stems and leaves with emergent spikes of pink flowers. *P. natans* and *P. coccineum* are the most common species. They provide food for aquatic wildfowl and muskrats.

126a (123) **Leaves broadly oval, round or heart-shaped** 127

126b **Leaves elongate or elliptic-lanceolate** 130

127a **Leaves cordate or deltoid** 128

127b **Leaves orbicular or round-reniform, sometimes peltate** 129

128a **Leaves deltoid; plant a sprawling, semiwoody vine with purple flowers which are borne in leaf axils; stamens exerted from recurved petals; fruit a red berry; plants of lake margins (Nightshade). Fig. 76** .... *Solanum* (Also see *Heteranthera limosa* (Fig. 94), leaves somewhat cordate.)

128b **Leaves deltoid to cordate; plants of bogs, not semi-woody vines; flowers small, numerous, in a spike enclosed by a white spathe (Water Arum). Fig. 69** .... *Calla*

129a (127) **Leaves broadly oval to nearly round in the upper part of the plant, petioles short, blades deeply lobed and compound in the lower part; flowers small and white, in heads or racemose; plants sprawling and procumbent to erect, often rank, the stems hollow; flowers with 4 petals and 6 stamens (Water Cress). Fig. 75** .... *Nasturtium*

129b **Leaves orbicular, broadly reniform or peltate, on long petioles from a procumbent stem; flowers in umbels; leaves usually serrate or crenate but sometimes nearly entire (Water Pennywort). Fig. 68** .... *Hydrocotyle* (Also see *Heteranthera reniformis* (Fig. 94) leaves reniform.)

130a (126) **Flowers 2-lipped, the upper usually split or divided, solitary on a short stalk in the axils of leaves or bracts (Lobelia). Fig. 81** .... *Lobelia*

Figure 81

Figure 81　*Lobelia dortmanna* (Lobeliaceae).
A. Habit of plant; B. Leaf in cross section
(diagrammatic).

This genus has several representatives in moist
situations and one especially (*L. dortmanna*)
is emergent in shallow water. This species has
a basal rosette of uniquely-shaped, fingerlike
leaves. The showy cardinal flower *L. cardinalis* is not aquatic but is found in swamps and
swales in the eastern half of the United States.

130b Flowers and leaves otherwise **131**

131a Leaves petiolate **140**

131b Leaves sessile **132**

**132a Plants prostrate or sprawling, some
branches erect** **133**

132b Plants definitely erect **136**

**133a Flowers arranged in close heads in the
axils of bracts, the stalks of the heads
arranged to form an umbel; leaves oblanceolate, sometimes entire but usually coarsely toothed (Eryngo). Fig. 78**
.... *Eryngium*

133b Flowers arranged otherwise **134**

**134a Flowers blue, salverform or rotate, with
a yellow center (flowers sometimes
white or pink), arranged to form a uni-
lateral raceme; leaves linear or oblanceolate (sometimes spatulate) (Forget-
me-not). Fig. 82** .... *Myosotis*

Figure 82

spicuous, solitary in the axils of leaves; calyx elongate (Water Primrose). Fig. 83 .... *Jussiaea* (Some authors regard *Jussiaea* as synonymous with *Ludwigia*. 47, Fig. 51.)

Figure 83 *Jussiaea* (Onagraceae) A. *Jussiaea decurrens*, habit; B. Flower; C. Decurrent leaves; D. *J. diffusa*, portion of stem.

These plants live both in shallow water or sprawl on shores. Flowers are yellow and showy, with long, slender, inferior ovaries. The common *J. decurrens* has lanceolate leaves from the base of which ridges extend down the stem. *Jussiaea* is found mostly in midwest and southern states.

Figure 82 *Myosotis* (Boraginaceae) A. Habit of plant; B. Flowers.

The familiar Forget-Me-Not is recognizable by its bright blue or pink flowers with yellow centers. Plants sprawl in shallow water or grow profusely in wet ditches and springy places. The numerous, dark seeds are used by birds.

134b Flowers shaped and arranged otherwise **135**

135a Leaves broadest near the base, narrowly to bluntly pointed, sessile and with or without ridges running down the stem from the leaf base; flowers yellow, con-

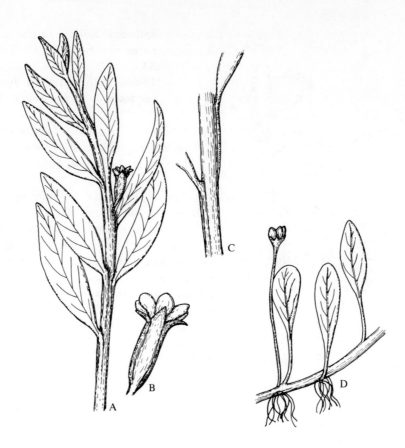

Figure 83

135b Leaves tapered at the base, sometimes forming a petiole; flowers whitish-green, pink or yellow; calyx short and urn-shaped; stems frequently rooting from the nodes; without wings or ridges extending down from leaf bases; leaves alternate in some but usually opposite (False Loosestrife). Fig. 51 .. *Ludwigia*

136a (132) Flowers yellow 137

136b Flowers purple, blue or white 138

137a Leaves glandular-dotted; flowers yellow with purple dots; solitary in the axils of leaves or in a terminal raceme; petals united at the base of a superior ovary (Loosestrife. Fig. 44 .... *Lysimachia*

137b Leaves not glandular-dotted; flowers always solitary in the axils of leaves; ovary inferior; fruit an elongated capsule; plants rank herbs, up to 2 M high (Water Primrose). Fig. 83 ...... *Jussiaea*

138a (136) Low (1 to 2.5 mm high) herbs with white (sometimes lavender) flowers arranged in a raceme or corymb; leaves simple on the upper part of the stem but pinnate, lobed or incised be-

low (Bitter Cress). Fig. 74 ....
.... *Cardamine*

138b Plants otherwise 139

139a Plants tall herbs, up to 2 M, semi-woody; leaves lanceolate, with the bases lobed, sessile; flowers purple with 6 petals, arranged in long, terminal spikes or solitary in the axils of leaves, or in whorls; capsule subcylindric (Spiked Loosestrife). Fig. 45 .... *Lythrum*

139b Plants not tall herbs, not semi-woody; leaves elliptic, nearly sessile, with spines in the axils; flowers blue, rotate, with 5 petals; capsule globular. Fig. 84 ....
.... *Hydrolea*

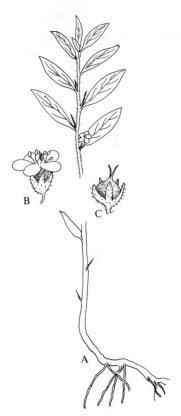

Figure 84

Figure 84 *Hydrolea* (Hydrophyllaceae) A. *Hydrolea quadrivalvis*, habit; B. Flower; C. Fruit.

In this genus the leaves are ellipsoid and alternate, somewhat similar to those of certain species of *Ludwigia* (Figure 51). There are spines in the axils of the leaves and there are other characters which separate it from *Ludwigia*. Flowers are blue, in 2's and 3's, borne in the axils of leaves. The three reported species of *Hydrolea* are distributed mostly in south central and southeastern states.

140a (131) Coarse, but smooth herbs up to 3 or even 9 M tall; leaves lanceolate to nearly ovate, the margins entire; flowers in panicles which are either terminal or axillary in leaves; dioecious; pistils with 2 to 5 long, plumose stigmas which persist; fruit a utricle (Water Hemp). Fig. 85 .... *Acnida*

Figure 85

Figure 85 *Acnida* (Amaranthaceae) A. *Acnida cannabina,* habit; B. Flower.

These are very tall, branched, non-woody annuals, but smooth and sometimes succulent. At least one variety is procumbent rather than erect. The elliptic leaves have petioles up to twice the length of the blade. Plants are dioecious. Flowers occur in very short panicles in the axils of the leaves. Two or three species are known for the United States, common in salt marshes and waste lands in southeastern and south central states.

140b Herbs otherwise; flowers not as above 141

141a Leaves slender, elongate (lanceolate or linear), entire but often on the same plant with leaves that may be serrate or toothed, or divided; flowers yellow; pistils numerous, forming achenes (Buttercup). Fig. 71 .... *Ranunculus*

141b Plants otherwise 142

142a Flowers solitary in the axils of leaves which are ovate or elliptic, margins smooth (False Loosestrife or Water-primrose). Figs. 51, 83 .... (*Jussiaea*) *Ludwigia*

142b Flowers forming a corymb or a terminal raceme (Bitter Cress). Fig. 74 .... *Cardamine*

143a (122) Leaves circular in outline, orbicular or reniform, sometimes peltate 144

143b Leaves elongate, lanceolate or long-elliptic 146

144a Leaves usually 3-lobed, sometimes very little divided and nearly entire, but with serrate or sharply crenate margins, variable on the same plant; flowers yellow or white, petals 5 or variable; pistils numerous, forming achenes when mature (Buttercup). Fig. 71 .... *Ranunculus* (*R. hederaceus et al.*)

144b Plants otherwise 145

145a Leaves circular or reniform, sometimes peltate, with coarsely or finely crenate margins, the round blades borne at the ends of long, vertical petioles from a subterranean, horizontal stem; flowers small, in umbels (sometimes much simplified); aquatic, with floating leaves, or terrestrial (Water Pennywort). Fig. 68 .... *Hydrocotyle*

145b Leaves nearly round or deltoid (sometimes with the base lobed), the margins sharply serrate; flowers yellow, with 5 to 9 petal-like sepals (petals lacking); pistils numerous, the fruit as thin-walled pods (follicle) (Marsh Marigold). Fig. 70 .... *Caltha*

146a (143) Plants submersed (some species with floating leaves); leaves alternate with a stipule, elongate-ellipsoid, slightly lobed at the base, narrowly or bluntly pointed at the apex; margin crisped and with minute serrations (Pondweed). Fig. 56 .... *Potamogeton crispus*

146b Plants otherwise 147

147a Plants with lower leaves deeply divided, incised or dissected (somewhat compound) 148

147b Plants with lower leaves not lobed or divided 151

148a Lower leaves finely dissected and compound, upper leaves simple, small, lanceolate or elliptic, sessile; flowers small, white in terminal racemes (Lake Cress). Fig. 73 .... *Neobeckia*

148b Plants with leaves and flowers otherwise 149

149a Lower leaves pinnately lobed, deeply incised and nearly compound; upper leaves serrate with sharply pointed apices; flowers small, solitary in the axils of leaves; calyx with 3 lobes, no petals; fruits small nutlets, 3-sided (Mermaid Weed). Fig. 77 .... *Proserpinaca*

149b Plants otherwise 150

150a Plants erect, little if at all branched; upper leaves narrowly elliptic to linear; lower leaves pinnately divided or compound; flowers small, greenish-yellow, in a terminal raceme; petals 4, stamens 6; fruit a globular silique, 2-chambered (Cress). Fig. 72 .... *Rorippa* (See note on p. 65)

150b Plants sprawling or much-branched; leaves elliptic or elongate-spatulate; flowers conspicuous, yellow, solitary on a peduncle; pistils many, forming achenes (Buttercup). Fig. 71 .... *Ranunculus*

151a (147) Flowers in dense heads, the heads stalked and arranged in umbels; leaves linear to lanceolate, lower coarsely serrate; plants tall and coarse (Eryngo). Fig. 78 .... *Eryngium*

151b Plants with a sheath at the base of the leaves; flowers pink-rose, or white, in whorls; leaves oval to lanceolate, crinkled and usually finely toothed (Dock). Fig. 79 .... *Rumex*

THE HOLDEN ARBORETUM
LIBRARY

152a (106) Plants floating 153

152b Plants rooted in the soil; submersed, emergent, or on shores 156

153a Leaves broad, lettucelike blades on a short, thick petiole from a thick stem that bears numerous, fine roots; stems proliferating by stolons and giving rise to secondary rosettes; (plants sometimes stranded on muddy shores); plants of tropical waters (Water Lettuce). Fig. 86 .... *Pistia*

Figure 86

Figure 86   *Pistia stratioides* (Araceae) Habit.

This plant is floating and lettucelike. Stranded plants wll grow well on muddy shores. The flowers are on a spadix with a light-colored spathe. The species is tropical or subtropical, occurring in the Gulf states and the extreme southwest United States. In some parts of the world *Pistia* becomes a serious nuisance to navigation (Panama Canal, *e.g.*).

153b Leaves otherwise 154

154a Leaves cordate or broadly elliptic 155

154b Leaf blades triangular in outline, pinnately lobed, or twice pinnate, arising from a floating rootstock that bears numerous roots; compound leaves pro-

ducing sporangia on the under side, the sporangia arranged in one or two rows on one or both sides of the longitudinal vein; (plants sometimes stranded on muddy shores); plants of tropical and subtropical waters (Floating Fern). Fig. 87 .... *Ceratopteris*

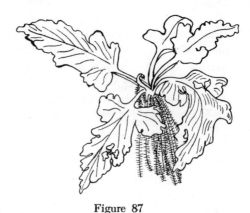

Figure 87

Figure 87   *Ceratopteris pteridoides* (Parkeriaceae) Habit of plant (redrawn from Muenscher).

This species and *C. Deltoides* are large, floating ferns of the Gulf region in the United States. The sterile leaves are triangular in outline and lobed; are borne in a rosette. The fertile fronds are pinnately compound. *C. pteridoides* has inflated petioles.

155a Leaves cordate, subcordate to broadly elliptic, up to 4 cm wide; blades with about 25 parallel veins all arising from the base of the blade and with conspicuous cross veins; blades spongy on the underside; flowers monoecious, staminate and pistillate both enclosed in a spathe with 2 bracts (Frogbit). Fig. 88 .... *Linnobium*

THE HOLDEN ARBORETUM
LIBRARY

Figure 88

Figure 88   *Limnobium spongia* (Hydrocharitaceae) Habit.

This plant may be either floating, or attached in mud. The heart-shaped leaves have characteristic, cross-hatched venation. It occurs along the Mississippi and Ohio rivers in central United States and along the Atlantic seaboard. The solitary flowers are on a recurved peduncle arising from a spathe.

155b Leaves with ovate or cordate blades on petioles which have an inflated, spongy bladder, the petioles arising from a short stem that proliferates by a stolon, secondary rosettes formed from the stolons; flowers violet to white and purple, irregular (somewhat zygomorphic), on a spike which arises from within a 2-valved spathe (Water Hyacinth). Fig. 89 .... *Eichhornia*

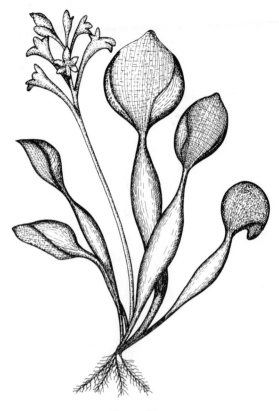

Figure 89

Figure 89   *Eichhornia crassipes* (Pontederiaceae) Habit.

This is the beautiful and infamous Water Hyacinth that dominates the water ways of the tropics and subtropics. The flowers are showy, light purple and white, arranged in a spike. The leaves have swollen petioles, forming floats that give great buoyancy. Plants multiply rapidly vegetatively wherever they become established. Water Hyacinth is used by aquatic animals for food, including the marine Manatee (Sea Cow). Water Hyacinth occurs in southeastern United States and has been reported from California.

156a (152) Small plants of bogs and acid, sandy soil; insectivorous; leaf blades circular or oval or filiform, bearing stiff hairs with glandular tips; leaves reddish; flowers white, in a panicle (Sundew). Fig. 90 .... *Drosera*

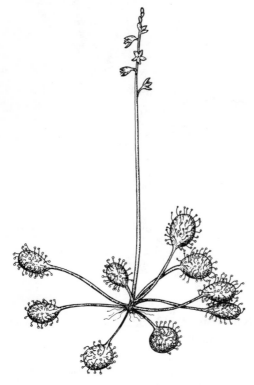

Figure 90

where Sundews live. One of the most common species is *D. rotundifolia* with circular or broadly oval leaves. *D. linearis* has long, slender, filiform leaves with scarcely any blade.

156b Plants otherwise 157

157a Leaves linear, fleshy, in a compact rosette, without petioles; flowering shoot naked, bearing 2-lipped flowers (Lobelia). Fig. 81 .... *Lobelia*

157b Plants with leaves otherwise 158

158a Leaves sagittate 159

158b Leaves with other shapes, orbicular, elliptic, (broadly elliptic in some), elongate-oval, lanceolate, linear, or triangular and pinnately lobed 161

159a Blades sharply arrow-shaped, with apex and basal lobes sharply pointed, with 3 prominent veins, a midvein and one extending into either lobe; petiole long and fleshy; flowers numerous, small, on a spike enclosed by a spathe (Arrow Arum). Fig. 91 .... *Peltandra*

Figure 90 *Drosera* (Droseraceae) Habit.

These small plants occupy *Sphagnum* bogs and sandy lake shores. The leaf blades and petioles bear glandular hairs. The sticky fluid produced by the hairs ensnares small insects and the hairs, being sensitive to touch, bend over and down, holding the insect until digestion has taken place, after which they regain their original position. It is thought that this type of nutrition aids in supplying nitrogen which is scarce or absent in the substrate

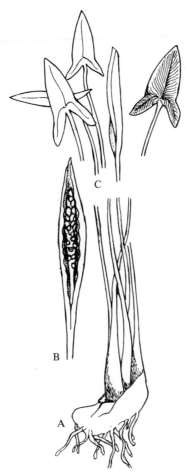

Figure 91

Figure 91 *Peltandra virginica* (Araceae) A. Basal portion of plant; B. Spadix and spathe; C. Leaves and spathe.

This is the widely distributed and familiar Arrow Arum of bogs, swamps and ditches. The leaves are superficially like those of *Sagittaria* but are readily differentiated by three prominent veins in the blade, one into either lobe, and one median. The inflorescence is distinctive, being a spadix with a spathe. This species is more common in the eastern half of the United States.

159b Leaves differently shaped and veined; flowers arranged otherwise **160**

160a Leaves with sagittate blades (elongate-lanceolate to linear when young and/or submersed); the petioles fleshy, veins several, of equal prominence, radiating from the base of the blade; flowers in whorls on a naked scape which is not inflated; lower flowers staminate or pistillate only, the upper flowers perfect; petals and sepals 3 (Arrowhead; Delta Potato). Fig. 92 .... *Sagittaria*

Figure 92 *Sagittaria* (Alismaceae) A. *Sagittaria cuneata;* B. *S. subulata;* C. *S. cristata;* D. Single flower; E. Head of fruits; F. *S. cristata;* G. Single nutlet; H. Leaf of *S. cuneata.*

Whereas most species have arrow-shaped blades, some have linear or ribbonlike leaves. Also some leaves are elliptical when plants are young and submersed but become sagittate in age. Others have grasslike leaves below the surface and elliptical blades when emergent. Species are submersed or emergent and form meadows in sloughs, lagoons and bayous. *S. latifolia* is the most widely distributed species. The plants bear underground tubers which are much sought after by ducks. The tubers (Delta Potatoes) are also used by Man for food. In especially favorable habitats *Sagittaria* may grow waist-high.

Figure 92

160b Leaves with sagittate blades but with
the lateral margins strongly convex;
veins arranged palmately from the base
of the blade; flowering scape inflated
and the pedicels of the flowers thick;
lower flowers perfect, upper flowers
with stamens only; sepals persisting and
closely enclosing the fruits which con-
sist of nutlets. Fig. 93 .... *Lophotocarpus*

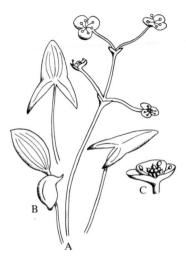

Figure 93

Figure 93 *Lophotocarpus* (Alismaceae) A. Portion of plant showing leaves and flowers; B. Fruit (nutlet); C. Lower, perfect flower.

In this genus the leaves are much the same in shape as *Sagittaria* and the plants grow in the same types of habitat. Leaves are often more lanceolate than sagittate. In *Sagittaria* the *lower* flowers in the raceme are pistillate, whereas in *Lophotocarpus* they are perfect. Some authors regard *Lophotocarpus* as synonymous with *Sagittaria*.

161a (158) Leaves cordate or reniform, sometimes with basal lobes reduced 162

161b Leaves not cordate or reniform, but orbicular, elliptical, elongate-lanceolate, or spatula-shaped; or broadly oval, ribbonlike and linear 166

162a Plants submersed; leaves broadly reniform, basal on a slender, creeping stem (but often alternate on an erect stem); flowers usually solitary (sometimes sev-

eral), in a spathe; leaves without a distinct midvein but with parallel veins from the leaf base (Mud Plantain). Fig. 94 .... *Heteranthera*

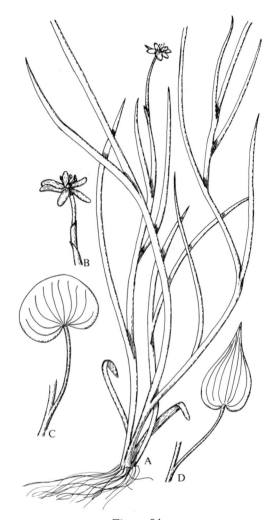

Figure 94

Figure 94 *Heteranthera* (Pontederiaceae) A. *Heteranthera dubia*, habit; B. Single flower; C. *Heteranthera reniformis*, leaf; D. *H. limosa*.

Heteranthera dubia is the most widely distributed of four species in the United States.

Plants often superficially resemble some *Potamogeton*. The leaves in some are linear and alternate but have no stipules. When in flower *Heteranthera* is readily differentiated by its starlike, trimerous flowers. Plants are used as food by ducks.

162b Plants otherwise **163**

163a Leaves broadly heart-shaped, the veins radiating from the base of the blade, several close together in the mid-region, forming a somewhat prominent rib; leaves clustered and located at the end of a prostrate rootstock; flowers in a spike and enclosed in a white spathe; plants of marshes and lagoon margins (Water Arum). Fig. 69 .... *Calla*

163b Leaves and flowers otherwise **164**

164a Leaves somewhat heart-shaped (but mostly lance-shaped) on long, erect, emergent petioles; blades with parallel veins, divergent from the base of the blade; flowers purple or blue, on a spike with a small basal spathe; stem a thickened pad, bearing many roots (Pickerelweed). Fig. 95 .... *Pontederia*

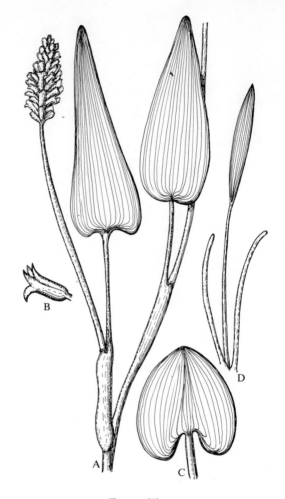

Figure 95

Figure 95 *Pontederia cordata* (Pontederiaceae) A. Habit of upper portion of plant; B. Single flower; C, D. Variation in shape of leaves.

This species has characteristic lance-shaped blades on long petioles with parallel venation. The flowering scape bears showy, bluish-purple blooms. The leaf petioles and flowering shoot are erect and emergent. Plants are used by muskrats and the seeds are eaten by many birds.

165a Leaves elliptic to slightly heart-shaped, blade with 25 or more parallel veins from the base, with many cross veinlets at right angles sometimes purple on the underside; plants proliferating by stolons; flowers monoecious, the staminate 3 to 10, in a spathe composed of 2 bracts; pistillate solitary or 2 in the same spathe; plants usually floating but sometimes attached (Frogbit). Fig. 88 ....
.... *Limnobium*

165b Leaves distinctly cordate, (submersed leaves lanceolate) the blade with 7 veins radiating from the base, the veinlets at right angles and forming rectangular spaces; flowers perfect on a pedicel which is part of a compound panicle (sometimes a simple one); flowers with up to 30 stamens and numerous pistils which form achenes that have an apical beak (Burhead). Fig. 96 ....
.... *Echinodorus*

Figure 96

Figure 96 *Echinodorus* (Alismaceae) A. Inflorescence (scape) and basal portion of *Echinodorus cordifolius;* B. Fruit.

In this genus the emergent leaves are heart-shaped and basal, submersed leaves lanceolate. The flowers form heads, borne on the branches of a panicle. The habit of growth is much like that of *Alisma* but differs by having flowers in heads rather than in rings about a receptacle. The fruits are used by waterfowl.

166a (161) Leaves fleshy, somewhat triangular in outline, becoming pinnately lobed or compound in age; ferns with sporangia on the back of pinnately compound, fertile fronds when mature, the sterile leaves broad, up to 4 dm long, the fertile pinnae narrow; margins of fronds bearing buds or developing plantlets; plants of tropical or subtropical waters (Floating Fern, Horn Fern). Fig. 87 .... *Ceratopteris*

166b Plants otherwise; not ferns **167**

167a Leaves round in outline or somewhat rhomboid, sagittate or peltate **168**

167b Leaves elliptic, elongate, lanceolate, oblong or ovate-elliptic, sometimes large, up to 3 feet long; spatulate or linear **170**

168a Leaves rhomboid or sometimes triangular, or nearly circular all on the same plant with leaves which are sagittate; flowers small, on a spike enclosed by a spathe; blades with 3 prominent veins, a midvein and a downwardly directed lateral vein into either lobe (Arrow Arum). Fig. 91 .... *Peltandra*

168b Plants otherwise **169**

169a Leaves circular, orbicular, sometimes peltate, with crenate margins; blades on long petioles from subterranean stems; flowers small, in umbels (Water Pennywort). Fig. 68 .... *Hydrocotyle*

169b Leaves nearly circular but mostly broadly reniform; margins serrate (entire in some species); flowers mostly solitary or 2, 3 together on a flowering shoot, sepals yellow or white (petals

lacking) (Marsh Marigold). Fig. 70 .... *Caltha*

170a (167) Plants low herbs with lanceolate or elongate-elliptic leaves on long petioles, margins crenulate, arising from the end of a horizontal, perennial rhizome; flowers solitary, white; leaves mostly in a basal rosette, but with some leaves on the stem; plants of marshes and sandy soil shores (Violet). Fig. 97 .... *Viola*

Figure 97

Figure 97 *Viola lanceolata* (Violaceae) Habit.

Although not truly aquatic some species of violet grow in marshes and on sandy shores. *V. lanceolata*, a white-flowered species is widely distributed in eastern United States whereas a subspecies occurs in western United States.

170b Plants otherwise; leaves shaped differently **171**

171a Plants dwarfed, up to 4 or 5 cm high; stem creeping, white runners giving rise to tufts of spatula-shaped leaves (sometimes linear in certain species) rounded at the tips; petioles long, slender, broadened apically into an elliptic blade; flowers solitary on simple, recurved peduncles (Mudwort). Fig. 98 .... *Limosella*

171b Plants larger; with leaves different .. 172

172a Leaf blades broadly elliptic or ovate on short, thick petioles; leaves up to 1 M long; inflorescence a spadix with a yellow or purple-spotted spathe 173

172b Leaves otherwise, smaller; stem often cormlike; inflorescence not a spadix ....
.... 174

173a Leaves broadly oval, on a short petiole, up to 6 dm long; spadix short at first, enclosed in a purple-spotted or striped spathe, elongating at maturity and bearing a globular or oval head of fruits, the spadix appearing before the leaves; plants with a skunk odor (Skunk Cabbage). Fig. 99 .... *Symplocarpus*

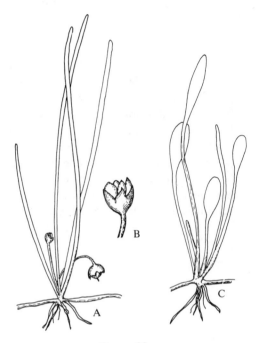

Figure 98

Figure 98 *Limosella* (Scrophulariaceae) A. *Limosella subulata*, habit; B. Single flower; C. *L. aquatica*, habit.

Species in this genus are dwarf plants with linear, flat or threadlike leaves. They live in mud; have runners which give rise to trufts of leaves, and root frequently. Each plant has three or four nodding stalks from the base that bear a single, small flower. Plants are rare but *L. aquatica* is widely distributed.

Figure 99

Figure 99 *Symplocarpus foetidus* (Araceae) Habit.

In this genus the leaves are broad, ovoid and basal arising from a perennial rootstock. The flowers are borne in a spadix and inclosed by a purplish spotted spathe, the spadix often appearing before the leaves in the spring. The common name Skunk Cabbage is derived from the fact that the leaves when crushed give off a distinct skunklike odor. Plants inhabit swamps and marshes. *S. foetidus* is distributed throughout the eastern half of the United States.

173b **Leaves broadly elliptic to oblanceolate and broadly oval, up to 1 M in length, the blades borne on stout petioles; spadix short and scarcely emergent at first, enclosed in a yellow spathe, eventually becoming elongate and clublike, bearing a cylindrical spike of fruits; plants with a skunk odor (Yellow Skunk Cabbage). Fig. 100** .... *Lysichitum*

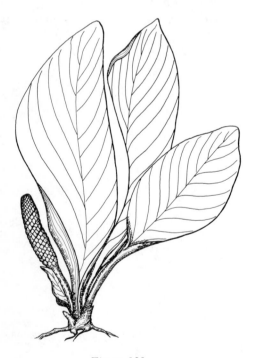

Figure 100

Figure 100 *Lysichitum americanum* (Araceae) Habit.

This is the Yellow Skunk Cabbage, a plant of bogs and marshes in northwestern North America. The leaves are broadly oval and large, up to 1.5 meters in length, all basal and arising from a rhizome. The spadix is enclosed at first in a yellow spathe but later enlarges remarkably and forms a club 3 or 4 dm in length.

174a (172) **Leaves elongate-lanceolate to somewhat spatulate, on a long, slender petiole which is inflated at the base, the blade with 3 veins or nerves, leaves all basal and arising from cormlike rootstocks; flowers white, with 3 sepals and petals, arranged in a panicle, 6 carpels forming achenes; leaves either submersed or with floating blades (Damasonium). Fig. 101** .... *Damasonium*

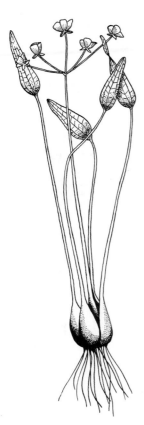

Figure 101

Figure 101 *Damasonium californicum* (Alis-maceae) Habit.

This is one of two genera in the Alismaceae in which the pistils (achenes) are arranged in a ring about the flower receptacle. The basal leaves are similar to those of *Alisma* in shape. The achenes, unlike *Alisma*, are conspicuously ridged on the *back*. Further, the petals are toothed rather than entire. Plants grow in shallow water (become emergent) or on shores.

174b Plants otherwise **175**

175a Leaves oblong-elliptic or sometimes lanceolate, rarely nearly cordate; blades with 1 prominent midvein and several lateral subparallel veins (3 on each side of the midvein), leaves all arising basic-ally from a cormlike stem; petioles often reddish; flowers small in compound pan-icles, with 3 white petals; numerous pis-tils on a flat receptacle, forming achenes which have a keel along one side and flattened on the other two sides (Water Plantain). Fig. 102 .... *Alisma*

Figure 102

Figure 102   *Alisma plantago-aquatica* (Alismaceae) A. Habit; B. Flowers; C. Fruits arranged around the receptacle; D. Nutlet of *Alisma gramineus;* E. Leaf of *A. gramineus;* F. *A. plantago-aquatica,* another leaf shape.

The most common species is *Alisma plantago-aquatica* with cordate or broadly elliptic leaves. *A. gramineus* has narrowly elliptic or linear leaves and is less common. Like *Damasonium,* the achenes are arranged in a ring about the receptacle, the achenes being smooth rather than ridged on the back, but with a keel on the side. Birds make limited use of the fruits for food.

175b Plants otherwise **176**

176a Leaves shaped somewhat like those of *Alisma,* **distinctly elliptic to lanceolate, the blade with about 10 longitudinal, subparallel veins of equal prominence, leaves all arising basally from a short, thick rootstock; flowers many, small on a spike which is naked (inconspicuous spathe); plants on shores or in shallow water (Golden Club). Fig. 103** .... *Orontium*

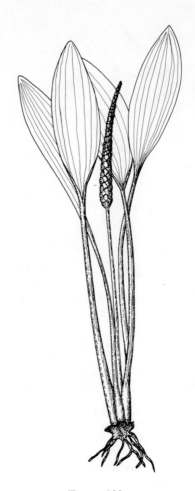

Figure 103

Figure 103   *Orontium aquaticum* (Araceae) Habit.

This species occurs in eastern United States especially along the coast where plants occupy ponds and tidal flats. The leaves are elongate-lanceolate on long petioles and the spadix is elongate-cylindric up to 2 dm long, arising from an inconspicuous spathe. Its yellow color accounts for the common name.

176b Plant with leaves and flowers otherwise **177**

177a Leaves linear, with some lanceolate blades which in some varieties are more often spatulate or elongate-cordate, all basal from a horizontal rootstock, the flowers funnelform, 2-lipped, blue-purple in a terminal cluster on a flowering shoot which bears a single head; petioles stout, erect, emergent in shallow water (Pickerelweed). Fig. 95 .... *Pontederia*

177b Plants with different leaves and flowers 178

178a Plants submersed, leaves ovate, or with parallel margins and without a distinct midrib, basal from near the end of a creeping rootstock (but often on the erect stem, and alternate); flowers solitary or 2, 3 together with a spathe (Mud Plantain). Fig 94 .... *Heteranthera*

178b Plants otherwise 179

179a Leaves, especially when young and submersed, elongate-ellipsoid or lanceolate to nearly linear, emergent; or older leaves sagittate, the petiole expanded toward the base and sheathing; flowers in whorls of 3, either on short stalks from a shoot, or on elongate stalks which are arranged in a whorl; lower flowers pistillate, upper flowers staminate (Arrowhead; Delta Potato). Fig. 92 .... *Sagittaria*

179b Leaves lanceolate or occurring as phyllodia when submersed, emergent leaves cordate; veins several, prominent, parallel from the base of the blade; flowers in an open panicle, the verticils bearing flowers in whorls; all flowers perfect; petals 3, pistils numerous, forming

achenes with a nearly erect apical beak (Burhead). Fig. 96 .... *Echinodorus*

180a (46) Leaves basal, appearing as clumped, several arising from a subterranean rootstock or rhizome 181

180b Leaves alternate, opposite or whorled, arising from the stem (although there may be some leaves at or near the base of the stem) 183

181a Leaves palmately compound 182

181b Leaves twice pinnately compound, a fern with both fertile and sterile leaves, or with one portion of the leaf fertile and another section sterile; plants of marshes, up to 1 M tall (Royal Fern). Fig. 104 .... *Osmunda*

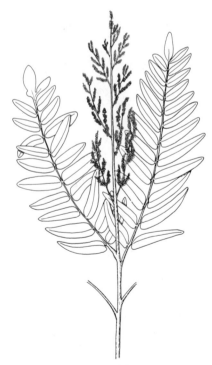

Figure 104

Figure 104 *Osmunda* (Osmundaceae) Habit of *Osmunda regalis* leaves and sporophylls.

This fern forms large clumps in swamps and bogs. The leaves are pinnately compound. Some species have sporangia borne on separate, chlorophylless leaves; others have special pinnae of vegetative leaves differentiated as reproductive leaflets. Rootstocks are perennial and long-lived, sometimes building sizeable mounds in swampy lands.

182a Leaves 2 or 3 from the end of a spongy rootstock; flowers white or pink, in a raceme on a leafless stalk; corolla funnelform, hairy; plants of marshes, especially in acid bogs with *Sphagnum* (Bog Bean, Buck Bean). Fig. 105 .... *Menyanthes*

Figure 105 *Menyanthes trifoliata* (Menyanthaceae; Gentianaceae) A. Habit of portion of plant; B. Single flower.

This species has relatively large, characteristically 3-lobed, compound basal leaves. The many-flowered stalk bears showy, white blooms. The fruit is a capsule, containing a number of brown seeds. The only species is widely distributed over the world, occurring in the eastern and far western parts of the United States.

182b Leaves 2 or 3 (rarely solitary) from a slender rhizome or a shortened rootstock, blade quadrifoliate on a slender petiole, especially long when submersed; plants short and matted when growing on shore; a nutletlike sporocarp borne laterally on the petioles when mature (Pepperwort). Fig. 106 .... *Marsilea*

Figure 105

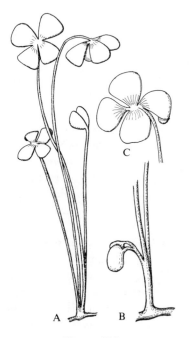

Figure 106

Figure 106 *Marsilea quadrifolia* (Marsileaceae) A. Habit of plant; B. Sporocarp lateral on leaf petiole; C. Leaf.

This is an aquatic fern which has 4-foliate, palmately compound leaves—appearing as an *Oxalis* or Shamrock. The petioles are long, especially when plants are aquatic. On land the plants are short-tufted, forming a turf. When plants are mature the petioles bear stalked sporangiophores which are used by water fowl. There are four species in the United States, of which *M. vestita* in the western half of the United States, and *M. quadrifolia* in the east are the most common. Plants often form a "lawn" on lakes shores, reproducing rapidly by proliferation from horizontal rootstocks.

183a (180) **Leaves alternate** **184**

183b **Leaves opposite or whorled** **207**

184a **Leaves compound, sparsely dichotomously branched to form thick, linear segments which are either tapering or flattened, olive or reddish-green; plants of streams, attached to rocks (River Weed). Fig. 107** .... *Podostemum*

Figure 107

Figure 107 *Podostemum ceratophyllum* (Podostemaceae) A. Habit of plant; B. Spathe and flower.

This is a distinctly shaped plant attached to rocks in flowing water. The leaves are stem-like, dichotomously divided, either long and slender, or short with flattened extensions. Stipules are frequently present at the base of the long petioles. *P. ceratophyllum*, with several varieties is the only species, occurring in western and southern United States. Plants are of biological importance in aquatic habitats, especially in reference to insect life histories.

184b **Plants with leaves otherwise** **185**

185a **Leaves palmately compound, 4-parted blades on long petioles, solitary from slender, horizontal rhizomes; (leaves** somewhat tufted, 2 or more arising together or seemingly so from the same point on the rhizome); leaflets triangular, the margins entire (rarely somewhat undulate) (Pepperwort). Fig. 106 .... *Marsilea*

185b Leaves pinnately compound or abundantly dichotomously divided 186

186a Leaves finely dissected into threadlike divisions 199

186b Leaves pinnately compound; blades flat although segments may be narrow; not finely dissected into filiform divisions 187

187a Leaves once-pinnate, with leaflets sometimes again deeply lobed 188

187b Leaves twice-pinnate 197

188a Leaves all basal, in a rosette; leaflets obovate or lanceolate, silvery below; plants of marshes and beaches; flowers yellow (Cinquefoil). Fig. 108 .... *Potentilla anserina*

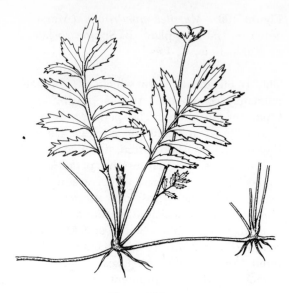

Figure 108

Figure 108 *Potentilla anserina* (Rosaceae) Habit, showing stolon.

This species has tufts of basal, pinnately compound leaves growing from runners. The plants occupy beaches, often among sedges. Flowers are yellow and buttercuplike. Because of their habit of growth these plants are useful in soil-binding and in beach-building. *P. pacifica* common in coastal marshes has glabrous leaves.

188b Leaves borne on procumbent or erect stems, not all basal 189

189a Plants with erect stems; branches none or few 192

189b Plants procumbent or sprawling, often much-branched 190

190a Leaves usually with 5 leaflets, that are elliptical or oblong lanceolate, the margins serrate, petioles with stipules which

sheath or clasp the stem; petioles red-purple; flowers solitary, purple and showy (Cinquefoil). Fig. 109 ....
.... *Potentilla palustris*

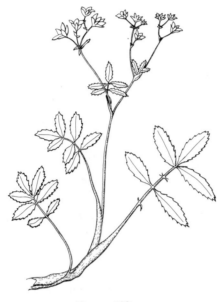

Figure 109

Figure 109   *Potentilla palustris* (Rosaceae) Habit of plant.

This species sprawls on shores and into the water, especially within reed beds and among cattail. The leaves are pinnately compound with purple petioles. The flowers also are purple. Both plants and seeds are known to be used by browsing animals and birds.

190b Plants otherwise 191

191a Plants with leaves that have 5 or 7 leaf-lets that are oval, with smooth margins; flowers white, small, many in somewhat compact racemes; petals 4, stamens 6; sprawling plants often with rank, hol-low stems (Water Cress). Fig. 75 ....
.... *Nasturtium*

191b Leaves 3 or 5-lobed, the lobes divided or coarsely toothed, the petioles with an expanded base; flowers yellow, usually solitary; petals 5 (sometimes more); pis-tils numerous, forming achenes; plants either hairy or glabrous (Buttercup). Fig. 71 .... *Ranunculus*

192a (189) Pinnately compound leaves in the lower part of a stem which has alternate, elliptic and coarsely serrate leaves above; flowers small, solitary in the axils of leaves (Mermaid Weed) Fig. 77 ......
.... *Proserpinaca*

192b Plants otherwise 193

193a Flowers yellow, solitary; petals 5 or sometimes variable; pistils numerous, forming achenes in a head (Buttercup). Fig. 71 .... *Ranunculus*

193b Plants otherwise 194

194a Flowers small, white, numerous, ar-ranged in an umbel 195

194b Plants otherwise 196

195a Fruit ellipsoid or oval, with 1 oil tube between pairs of ridges; plants low, 0.5 to 1.8 dm tall; leaflets narrowly oblong with serrate margins (sometimes entire) (Dropwort; Hog-fennel). Fig. 110 ....
.... *Oxypolis*

Figure 110

Figure 110 *Oxypolis occidentale* (Umbelliferae) A. Habit of plant portion; B. Fruit; C. Cross section of fruit.

This species occurs in western United States, especially in subalpine regions, either in shallow water or in grassy bogs. Three other species are found in eastern and southern states. The plants have fascicles of fleshy roots. *Oxypolis* is often distinctive because at least some of the upper leaves are reduced to spikelike phyllodes (blades lacking). The basal leaves are pinnately compound with five to 13 leaflets. They occur along streams and in marshes.

195b Fruit oblong, with 2 oil tubes between pairs of ridges; flowers white in compound umbels; lower submersed leaves highly dissected (Water Parsnip). Fig. 111 .... *Sium*

Figure 111

Figure 111 *Sium suave* (Umbelliferae) Habit showing variations in leaf divisions.

This species is nearly always aquatic and emergent; many times growing in meadows and marshes where there is standing water. The lower leaves are variously divided, sometimes filiform, whereas the upper, emergent leaves have broad, pinnately compound blades. Whereas the plants probably play a role in aquatic biology as an aerator there seems to be no use by animals or birds. The species is widely distributed over the United States.

196a (194) Flowers yellowish-green, in a raceme or panicle (Cress). Fig. 72 .... *Rorippa*

196b Flowers white (or lavender), in a raceme (Bitter Cress). Fig. 74 .... *Cardamine*

197a (187) Plants prostrate or procumbent, rooting from the nodes: leaves mostly twice-pinnate (occasionally some once-pinnate); the leaflets broadly ovate with coarsely serrate margins, 2 to 6 cm long; flowers white, in terminal, compound umbels; fruit oblong cylindric, with 1 oil tube between each pair of ridges (Water Celery). Fig. 112 .... *Oenanthe*

198a Tall, rank plants up to 3 M high; leaves coarse, thick, twice-pinnate lower leaves sometimes ternate), broad and up to 4 dm long; leaflets lanceolate or linear-elliptic; coarsely serrate, up to 8 cm long; fruit globular, but laterally compressed; umbels numerous, their involucres relatively small and inconspicuous, or lacking (Water Hemlock). Fig. 113 .... *Cicuta*

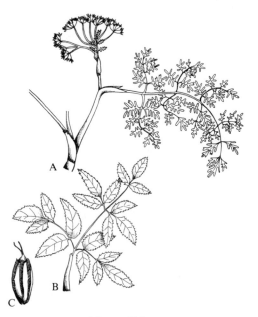

Figure 112

Figure 112 *Oenanthe* (Umbelliferae) A. Habit of upper portion of plant; B. Lower leaf; C. Fruit.

This is a distinctly aquatic genus in the family. The plants are mostly procumbent but have erect branches. The leaves are twice-compound. *O. saementosa* is found in habitats along the northwest Pacific coast.

197b Plants erect **198**

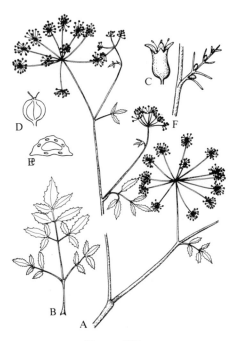

Figure 113

Figure 113 *Cicuta bulbifera* (Umbelliferae) A. Habit of upper portion of plant; B. Lower leaf; C. Flower; D. Fruit; E. Cross section of Fruit.

This species is more widely distributed than *C. maculata*, both species growing in shallow water or in swales. Like *Oxypolis* there are fleshy roots. Plants are large, usually erect with dense umbels of white flowers, and with twice-pinnately or ternately compound leaves. This is the famous Water Hemlock with poisonous roots.

198b Plants up to 1 1/2 M tall, usually much less; leaves thin, the divisions spreading widely, the leaflets oval or ovate-lanceolate; the umbel of flowers relatively large with 20 to 45 stalks, variable in length; involucre conspicuous (Angelica). Fig. 114 .... *Angelica*

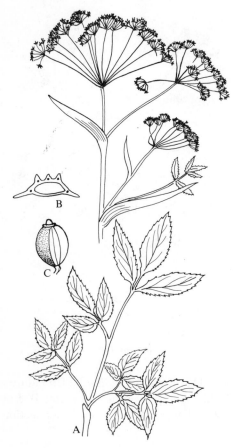

Figure 114

Figure 114 *Angelica* (Umbelliferae) A. Leaves and umbels in upper portion of plant; B. Cross section of fruit; C. Fruit.

In this genus the leaves are twice-pinnate or ternately compound, and with leaflets broader than in *Cicuta*. The sheaths at the base of the leaves are relatively long, up to 10 cm, whereas in *Cicuta* they are only 3 cm or less. The plants are tall, up to 2 M. *Angelica* is one of the genera in the Umbelliferae which has fruits with winged ribs. Like *Cicuta*, *Angelica* grows in marshes and along stream courses.

199a (186) Plants floating **200**

199b Plants attached, submersed or on the shore **201**

200a Stems stout, inflated, submersed portion bearing uncrowded, pinnately compound leaves, the emersed portion with a rosette of much-inflated branches, bearing whorls of small flowers (Featherfoil). Fig. 115 .... *Hottonia*

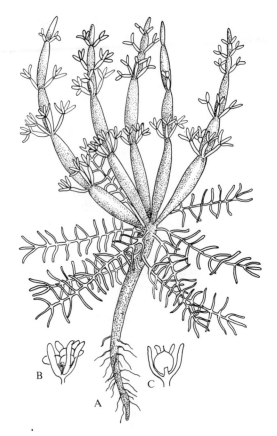

Figure 115

Figure 115 *Hottonia inflata* (Primulaceae)
A. Habit of plant; B. Flower; C. Fruit.

This is a unique, floating plant (rarely stranded). The thick, vertical axial stem has a rosette of inflated branches at the surface that bear whorls of flowers. The leaves are submersed and pinnately compound (somewhat rootlike), the divisions linear. In the United States the species is found in southern regions and in the Ohio valley.

200b Stems long, threadlike and lax, bearing alternate or opposite, finely dissected and dichotomously divided leaves that bear numerous animal-catching blad-

ders (Bladderwort). Fig. 116 ....
.... *Utricularia*

201a (199) Leaves dichotomously or irregular dissected to form threadlike divisions, the divisions sometimes flattened and narrowly ribbonlike 202

201b Leaves pinnately divided to form threadlike divisions 204

202a Leaves (and stem branches) bearing animal-trapping bladders, the bladders at first green and purplish, becoming black in age; flowers yellow or purple, 2-lipped, the lower lip with a spur; the flowers borne on erect, naked scapes (except for bracts at the base of flower peduncles); plants attached, anchored but without roots, or, more often, floating freely and drifting just beneath the water surface (Bladderwort). Fig. 116 .... *Utricularia*

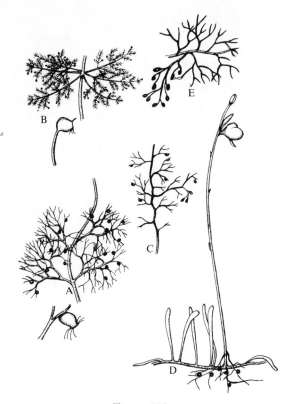

Figure 116

Figure 116 *Utricularia* (Lentibulariaceae)
A. *Utricularia vulgaris* leaves; B. *U. purpurea*
leaves and bladder; C. *U. minor* leaves; D. *U.
cornuta*, habit; E. *U. intermedia* branches with
bladders.

This genus is unique in its possession of bladders on finely dissected leaves, or on special,
slender branches, all of which are dichotomously divided. A few species have a horizontal, subterranean stem, a few erect branches
and flowering scapes. The plants are rootless
but may lie on the bottom, more often are freely floating. Flowers are yellow or purple. *Utricularia* is often found in acid or softwater habitats, although they do occur in basic waters.
The bladders have valvelike "doors" which
open to allow small animals to enter. Animals
are digested and contribute to the nitrogen

metabolism of the plant. The bladders are
green at first, become purple and then black
in age as insect remains collect in them. The
plants are often coated with adherent or epiphytic algae. Fourteen or 15 species are widely
distributed in the United States.

202b Leaves without bladders; plants other-
wise 203

203a Leaves alternate, but rarely so, mostly
opposite or whorled, without a sheath
at the base of the petiole, primary divisions palmate, successive divisions
dichotomous; stem often bearing oblong, peltate, floating leaves; flowers
solitary, white with 3 sepals and 3 petals,
carpels 3 or 4; flowers borne on a slender peduncle in the axils of some upper
leaves; fruit a 1-seeded, nutlike follicle
(Fanwort, Parrot Feather). Fig. 33 ......
.... *Cabomba*

203b Leaves alternate (rarely opposite), ulti-
mate divisions dichotomous although
the first divisions are palmate; plants
sometimes with upper or floating leaves
lobed or not so finely dissected as the
submersed leaves which have a sheath
at the base; flowers white or yellow,
petals 5 (or indefinite in number); pistils numerous, forming achenes (Buttercup). Fig. 71 .... *Ranunculus*

204a (201). Plants stout with hollow stems;
the basal leaves in a rosette (or whorl),
finely divided, the upper leaves pinnately compound or twice-pinnate, the
leaflets sometimes elliptic or lanceolate
in some forms; base of petiole expanded
to form a somewhat clasping sheath;
flowers small, white, in a terminal umbel; plants emergent or on boggy shores
(Water Parsnip). Fig. 111 .... *Sium*

204b Plants not as above **205**

205a Plants erect (at least in part), or trailing in the water, with tufted, pinnately compound, finely dissected leaves arranged along the entire length of the submersed portion of the stem; leaves on the emergent portion simple, elliptic, sessile and coarsely serrate; flowers white, in terminal racemes in the axils of the upper leaves; petals 4; fruit a 1-chambered, globular pod (Lake Cress). Fig. 73 .... *Neobeckia* (*Armoracia*)

205b Plants not as above **206**

206a Stems narrow, long, cordlike and lax, bearing alternate (or more often whorled), pinnately compound, feathery leaves with threadlike divisions; flowers small, inconspicuous, in whorls on the upper part of the stem, the whorls subtended by bracts which are either simple or pinnately lobed; the flower-bearing portion of the stem emergent (Milfoil). Fig. 117 .... *Myriophyllum*

Figure 117

Figure 117   *Myriophyllum* (Haloragaceae)
A. *Myriophyllum exalbescens,* habit of plant;
B. Flower; C. Leaf; D. *M. verticillatum.*

Plants of this genus form dense, submersed beds. They are rooted but are often found floating freely. When mature the flowering apices of the stems appear above the water surface. The whorled leaves are finely dissected and pinnately compound. One species (*M. tenellum*) has reduced, knoblike leaves only. There are nine species widely distributed in the United States. They are useful in aeration and as food for muskrat and moose; seeds are eaten by many kinds of birds.

206b   Stems stout, the upper branches in a whorl and inflated, the lower undivided portion of the stem bearing pinnately compound leaves which are longer than in *Myriophyllum;* flowers small, consisting of a calyx with 5 lobes and a 5-lobed corolla that has a short tube; the fruit a 5-valved capsule; flowers arranged in whorls on the inflated branches; plants often floating, sometimes rooted on muddy shores (Featherfoil). Fig. 115 .... *Hottonia*

207a   (183) Leaves opposite 208

207b   Leaves whorled 212

208a   Leaves finely dissected to form thread-like segments 209

208b   Leaves pinnately divided to form leaflets with flat blades 210

209a   Leaves sessile, the leaf divided into threads from the point of origin on the stem; emersed leaves elliptic, pinnately

lobed and coarsely serrate; inflorescence a head in which there are both ray flowers (marginal) and tubular flowers (central) (Compositae, Water Marigold). Fig. 63 .... *Megalodonta*

209b   Leaves with a petiole, the divisions arising at the end of a short stalk; emersed leaves oval, floating leaves with peltate blades; flowers white or yellow with 3 petals and sepals, borne singly on peduncles in the axils of leaves (Fanwort; Parrot Feather). Fig. 33 .... *Cabomba*

210a   (208) Leaves twice-divided, the primary divisions palmate, the secondary pinnately compound, usually alternate but sometimes opposite; stems hollow; flowers in umbels (Water Hemlock). Fig. 113 .... *Cicuta*

210b   Plants not as above 211

211a   Leaves pinnately or palmately compound, the leaflets elliptical, stalked, the margins coarsely serrate; lateral leaf veins straight to the margin; inflorescence a head (Compositae), terminal or axillary, the ray flowers sometimes wanting (Bur Marigold). Fig. 118 .... *Bidens*

Figure 118

Figure 118 *Bidens* (Compositae) Habit of plant.

Species of this genus live in wet meadows, marshes and swales; are sometimes marginal in shallow lake water. Some species occur in more arid situations. The composite type of inflorescence may or may not have ray flowers. The abundant fruits are used by many birds, both upland and aquatic. *Bidens* species are widely distributed in the United States.

211b Leaves pinnately and deeply lobed so as to appear compound, the divisions narrow and with entire margins; flowers greenish-white, solitary or borne 2, 3 together in the axils of leaves; plants covered with sticky hairs. Fig. 42 .... *Leucospora*

212a (207) Leaves dichotomously divided 213

212b Leaves pinnately compound (Milfoil). Fig. 117 .... *Myriophyllum*

213a Divisions of leaf with small but obvious marginal, hornlike projections; leaves 3 in a whorl (sometimes opposite), sessile; plants floating, not possessing roots but sometimes the stem embedded in muddy bottoms (Hornwort, Coontail). Fig. 119 .... *Ceratophyllum*

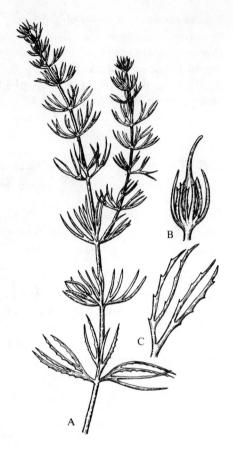

Figure 119

Figure 119   *Ceratophyllum* (Ceratophyllaceae) A. Habit of *Ceratophyllum demersum*;
B. Pistilate flower; C. Leaf.

This is the familar Coon Tail, so-called because of the densely bushy stem tips. Plants
are readily identified by the whorls of dichotomously forked leaves that have marginal
teeth or horns. This is one of the few genera
without roots. Plant stems may have a portion embedded in bottom sediments. The flowers and fruits are solitary in the axils of leaves,
showng as small, red cylinders. *Ceratophyllum* is only moderately efficient as an aerator,
but plants are much used by muskrats and by
birds.

213b Divisions of leaf without hornlike marginal projections 214

214a Leaves with conspicuous, glandlike
bladders, green when young, becoming
black in age; flowers purple (Bladder-
wort). Fig. 116 ....
.... *Utricularia purpurea*

214b Leaves without bladders. Fig. 33 ....
.... *Cabomba*

215a (37) Leaves in the form of hollow,
cylindrical petioles without blades, occurring on plants in which lower leaves
(when present) are pinnately compound, the leaflets broadly oval or orbicular in outline; flowers in compound
umbels (Dropwort). Fig. 110 ....
.... *Oxypolis*

215b Plants otherwise 216

216a Leaves small, green scales or bracts, or
sometimes reduced to merely knobs on
the stem, the leaves scattered or closely
arranged and overlapping 217

216b Leaves in the form of colorless (without chlorophyll) scales, teeth or bracts
.... 231

217a Leaves occurring as or appearing to be
lobes or joints; plants seemingly thal-
loid, floating 218

217b Plants otherwise 223

218a Joints linear or finger-like, solitary or clustered in a rosette, the segments downward directed from the water surface (Strap-shaped Duckweed). Fig. 5 .... *Wolffiella*

218b Plants otherwise 219

219a Plants consisting of 3 or 4 oval or circular lobes adjoining at their bases; each lobe bearing rootlets; lobes purple on the under side (Great Duckweed). Fig. 3 .... *Spirodela*

219b Plants otherwise 220

220a Plants consisting of 2 (or 3) oval lobes adjoining along one margin, each lobe bearing a single rootlet (Duckweed). Fig. 4 .... *Lemna*

220b Plants otherwise 221

221a Plants consisting of elongate, spatula-shaped lobes, arranged in a cross-shaped fashion, each lobe bearing a single root, plants floating in tangled clumps just below the water surface, or clustered about submersed aquatic plants (Star Duckweed). Fig. 4 .... *Lemna trisulca*

221b Plants otherwise 222

222a Plant consisting of one or more pairs of broadly oval to nearly circular leaves, attached to a short stem, the upper surface with stiff bristles; (a third submersed leaf arises from the ventral side of the stem at the same node as the one bearing the dorsal leaves, the ventral leaf highly dissected and rootlike, chlor-

ophylless, bears sporocarps when plants are mature); roots lacking (Water Fern; Floating Moss). Fig. 20 .... *Salvinia*

222b Plants consisting of several overlapping scalelike leaves which are usually red-tinged, the leaves possessing ventral lobes; leaves borne on a short, floating stem which has roots on the ventral surface (Water Velvet). Fig. 19 .... *Azolla*

223a (217) — Plants attached, submersed, emergent, or on shore with minute, scalelike leaves or bracts, remote and not over-lapping on the stem 224

223b Plants with leaves otherwise 225

224a Plants with inflated, succulent leaves, either herbaceous or (as perennials) semi-woody at the base and shrublike; leaves minute, opposite scales; flowers small, borne in the axils of the upper scales and forming a terminal spike; plants of ocean beaches and alkali lake shores (Glasswort). Fig. 120 .... *Salicornia*

Figure 120

Figure 120 *Salicornia* (Chenopodiaceae) Habit of plant.

Species of this genus are low, sprawling plants with some erect stems. They inhabit salt-water or alkali beaches, occurring just above the high-tide level. The stems are succulent but the base of perennial species may be somewhat woody and tough. The leaves are opposite but are reduced to scales or "knobs," sometimes showing only as a rim at the node.

224b Erect, almost naked stems or flowering scapes from a subterranean branch, bearing a few, bilobed showy flowers; leaves in the form of small scales which are united to form a tubelike collar about the stem, or as alternately arranged 3-parted bracts; (plants often have subterranean, colorless, club-shaped leaves and modified branches bearing animal-trapping glands) (Bladderwort). Fig. 116 .... *Utricularia*

225a (223) Plants with small leaves reduced to rounded knoblike members on upright stems, growing from submersed and subterranean, horizontal stems; flowers small and inconspicuous, in the axils of upper leaves (Milfoil). Fig. 121 .... *Myriophyllum tenellum*

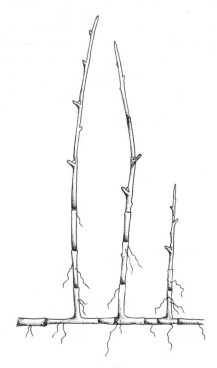

Figure 121

Figure 121 *Myriophyllum tenellum* (Haloragidaceae) Habit of plant showing knoblike leaves.

This is unlike other species in the genus because the leaves occur as alternate, knoblike scales. This plant grows on sandy shores or in shallow, marginal water, the creeping branches sending up naked stems.

225b Plants with green, narrow and linear, ovate or elliptic leaves, numerous on the stem **226**

226a Small (a few mm long) green leaves, opposite on the stem 227

226b Leaves alternate, usually crowded and overlapping 228

227a Plants prostrate and matted, or partially erect, rooting at the nodes; leaves obovate or spatula-shaped, 3-5 mm long to as much as 1 cm (in some species), lying against the ground in terrestrial species; flowers solitary, sessile in the axils of leaves; sepals and petals 2 to 4, pistils 2 to 81; fruit a minute capsule with thin walls (Waterwort). Fig. 53 .... *Elatine*

227b Dwarf plants which are tufted and erect or sometimes creeping, rooted at the base of the stem; leaves narrow, elongate bracts; flowers solitary on a short peduncle, axial in the leaves; petals and sepals 3 or 4 and as many stamens; fruit a follicle (Pigmy Weed). Fig. 52 .... *Tillaea*

228a (226) Leaves linear to filliform scales, alternate, with one vein, the apex of the leaf bidentate; stems prostrate and nearly covered by the overlapping leaves; flowers solitary in the axils of leaves; stamens and sepals 3, fruit a one-chambered capsule; plants floating or on shore (Pool Moss). Fig. 122 .... *Mayaca*

Figure 122

Figure 122 *Mayaca* (Mayacaceae) A. Habit of plant; B. Fruit.

The densely branched stems have numerous, small, scalelike leaves. The plants form floating mats and although it is a flowering plant it is well-named Pool Moss. The small, white or pink flowers are solitary on slender peduncles. There are two species in southern states. They are undoubtedly efficient aerators but there is no known biological importance.

228b Plants different; "leaves" oval, elliptic or nearly circular, often closely overlapping on procumbent, spreading "stems" (Mosses). 229

229a "Leaves" with a midrib 230

229b "Leaves" without a midrib, arranged in 3 rows, closely overlapping, often dark green or blackish, somewhat trough-shaped or with a keel. Fig. 16 .... *Fontinalis*

230a "Leaves" spirally arranged on an elongated, branched "stem," or in 2 rows, but spreading from all sides, sickle-shaped and curling, the apex of the "stem" with a curling tuft. Fig. 18 .... *Drepanocladus*

230b "Leaves" in 2 rows, spreading from 2 sides of the "stem," having a superficial plate of cells forming a pocket along one side of leaf at the base. Fig. 17 .... *Fissidens*

231a (216) Leaves in the form of chlorophylless teeth in a whorl at the nodes of branched, jointed green stems, the teeth black or brown; stems otherwise leafless and bearing terminal sporangiophores arranged in a cone; the stem fluted and rough to the touch because of silicon deposits (Horse Tail Fern). Fig. 123 .... *Equisetum*

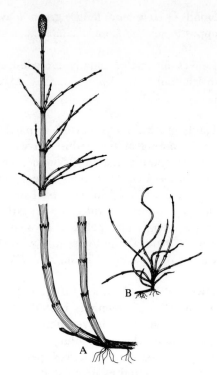

Figure 123

Figure 123 *Equisetum* (Equisetaceae) A. *Equisetum fluviatile*; B. *E. scirpoides*.

This is the familiar Horse Tail genus of fern-like plants. A few species are aquatic such as *E. fluviatile* or semi-aquatic, as are *E. scirpoides, E. littorale* and *E. palustre*. Plants have green, jointed and fluted stems which are leafless except for a whorl of chlorophylless scales at the joints. *E. fluviatile* is important in filling in of lakes. Dense meadows of the plant may occur in lagoons and bays. It is also important as food for muskrats. Some birds use the upper parts of the stems for grit because of the large quantity of silicon in the epidermal cell walls. Because of their hard texture *Equisetum* species have been used as scouring rushes by Indians.

231b Leaves club-shaped or spatula-shaped, on horizontal stem which may also bear modified branches that have animal-trapping glands; vertical branches bearing terminal flowers, the scape naked but with a few alternate or opposite scales (Bladderwort). Fig. 116 ....
.... *Utricularia*

232a (36) Plants with long, tapering, grass-like leaves with subparallel margins, clasping the stem, the blade bearing a liplike ligule at the base where the leaf forms its sheath (See *Triglochin*, Fig. 144 in the Juncaginaceae, however); leaves 2-ranked; stems hollow, round in cross section; flowers in spikelets* which are composed of 2 glumes (basal scales) above which are 1 or several florets, each floret composed of a lemma, a palea, a pistil and stamens (in rare instances flowers are monoecious, *Zizania, e.g.*; or dioecious as in some none-aquatic genera) (Grass Family, Gramineae) (see plate 1) 233

232b Plants otherwise; leaves without ligules
.... 240

233a Flowers in terminal panicles with those in the upper part pistillate, the spikelets closely arranged, those below staminate and more loosely arranged; (plants often submersed when young, the leaf blades floating on the surface) (Wild Rice; Indian Rice). Fig. 124 ...... *Zizania*

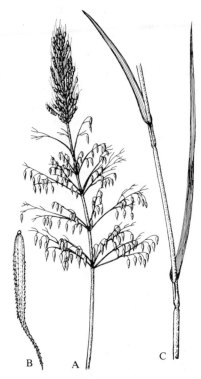

Figure 124

Figure 124   *Zizania aquatica* (Gramineae) A. Panicle of staminate (above) and pistillate (below) flowers; B. Achene; C. Stem and leaves.

This is a tall, aquatic grass of sloughs and lagoons which, because of its abundant, edible seed has been important in the economy and social life of Indian tribes. Seeds are harvested and sold commercially in Michigan, Wisconsin and Minnesota. The grains are highly useful to birds as food, and the dense stands make suitable nesting sites. Another species, *Z. texana* is rare, occurring only in Texas.

(*) See *Glyceria borealis* and *G. fluitans* (Fig. 127, submersed grasses, with ribbonlike leaves, which seldom flower except when emergent.)

233b Flowers with stamens and pistils in the same spikelet 234

234a Flowers in plumelike panicles which persist as feathery white tufts throughout the winter; plants canelike up to 4 M tall; leaves relatively broad and widely spreading from the stem; plants usually growing in dense stands in lake margins or in sloughs, wet ditches, etc. (Cane Grass). Fig. 125 ...... *Phragmites*

Figure 125

Figure 125 *Phragmites maximus* (Gramineae) A. Panicle; B. Leaf; C. Floret.

This tall, cane grass forms dense stands in quiet water of lake bays, in sloughs and in roadside ditches. It is important biologically as cover for birds and other small animals. The leaves are wide, up to 5 cm in large specimens. The stems bear dense panicles of flowers, the scales purple at first, but the numerous silky hairs of the spikelets produce conspicuous white plumes which persist throughout the winter months. The one species (and its varieties) is widely distributed over the United States.

234b Plants otherwise; shorter leaves; plants not so tall (up to 1 1/2 M); inflorescence not plumelike 235

235a Spikelet forming oval (but compressed) clumps on short lateral stalks, the clumps forming several rows and overlapping so as to form a rather compact panicle; spikelets arranged on more than one side, without spines; plants with many leaves, up to 1.5 M tall (Canary Reed Grass). Fig. 126 .... *Phalaris*

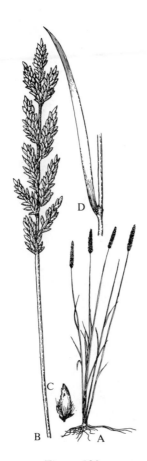

Figure 126

Figure 126 *Phalaris arundinacea* (Gramineae) A. Habit of plant; B. Panicle; C. Lemma; D. Stem and leaf.

This species occurs in dense clumps, with the flowering stems rising well above the leaves. Plants may be up to 1½ M tall. The spikelets are clumped and closely appressed so that a relatively firm, cylindrical inflorescence is produced. The leaves are relatively wide, up to 15 mm. Seeds are much used by birds. The species occurs throughout the United States, both in marginal aquatic and in dry situations.

235b Plants otherwise 236

236a Plants with erect stems growing from rhizomes; panicle usually loose and spreading, the spikelets sessile, compact or loose, with several flowers; the spikelets elliptic or ovate, not compressed; lemma ridged with 5 to 9 nerves; glumes unequal in length, shorter than the first lemma; leaf margins joined at the base to form a closed sheath; plants of marshes, forming dense meadows, or submersed with the long, narrow leaves (reddish) floating at the surface (submersed plants not flowering) (Manna Grass). Fig. 127 .... *Glyceria*

Figure 127

Figure 127 *Glyceria* (Gramineae) A. *Glyceria fluitans*, habit in submersed position; B. Panicle; C. Lemma; D. Spikelet; E. Stem and leaves.

This genus includes several species which are either aquatic or semi-aquatic, forming dense meadows and providing much food and cover for birds. Several species have spreading, loose panicles. *Glyceria fluitans* and *G. borealis* commonly grow submersed; have narrow, ribbonlike leaves floating out on the surface. These species seem never to produce flowers when submersed. The genus is distinctive in having a closed sheath (usually) at the base of the blade.

236b Plants otherwise; panicle different; stems from rhizomes or not **237**

237a Spikelets overlapping, all on one side **238**

237b Spikelets otherwise, compactly arranged in a cylindrical spike; glumes blunt-pointed but fringed dorsally; young spikes showing stamens conspicuously (Fox Tail Grass). Fig. 128 .... *Alopecurus*

Figure 128

Figure 128 *Alopecurus* (Gramineae) A. Habit of plant; B. Lemma and awn.

Species of this genus form rather sparse patches on the margins of lakes and in shallow water. They are relatively short, usually 2 or 3 dm tall. Spikes of flowers are dense, forming an inflorescence much like that of Timothy. The stamens are long and conspicuous showing red and yellow in the spikelet. *Alopecurus aequalis* is the most common and widely distributed; is useful as a soil binder.

**238a Spikelets with a fringed margin, over-
lapping, in one row (Cut Grass). Fig.
129** .... *Leersia*

Figure 129   *Leersia* (Gramineae) Habit of
plant.

This genus has overlapping spikelets and in
one row, giving a characteristic, one-sided appearance to the branches of the panicles. Two
species and their varieties are widely distributed on lake margins and in wet meadows.
Plants and seeds are used by both birds and
muskrats.

238b Spikelets in 2 rows **239**

Figure 129

239a Spikelets about as long as wide, in one-sided spikes that are about 3 times as long as wide (Slough Grass). Fig. 130 ....
.... ***Beckmannia***

Figure 130

Figure 130 *Beckmannia* (Gramineae) Habit of plant.

In this genus the spikelets form two rows on one side of the stem. The panicle is not open and loose but rather close, and is interrupted rather than continuous. *B. syzigachni* is found in suitable habitats throughout the United States, although apparently it does not occur in the Gulf region.

239b Spikelets elongate, the palea often tapering to a long point; spikes up to 12 times the width in length; plants tall, up to 1.5-2 M with many leaves that taper to narrowed apices, long and whip-like (Cord Grass). Fig. 131 .... ***Spartina***

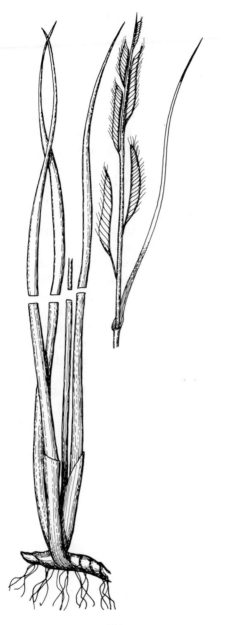

Figure 131

Figure 131 *Spartina pectinata* (Gramineae) Habit of plant.

This species of the genus grows rankly in sloughs, salt marshes and along beach mar-

gins. Plants may be as much as 2 M tall. The leaves are very long, coarse and rough, have a whiplike tip. The spikelets are compressed laterally and arranged in one-sided spikes which are erect. Other species are found in coastal marshes. All are important in erosion control and in soil-building, partly because the plants have large, cordlike rhizomes.

240a (232) **Plants with long, slender green stems, more than 10 times their diameter; leaves lacking or occurring as sheaths at the base of the stem** 241

240b **Plants with elongate leaves, either grasslike, ribbonlike, linear, linear-oblong to linear lanceolate** 244

241a **Leaves on the stem reduced, without blades, occurring as hollow petioles with basal leaves pinnately compound and with long petioles, the leaflets nearly circular or broadly ovate; flowers small, white, in an umbel (Dropwort). Fig. 110** .... *Oxypolis*

241b **Plants otherwise** 242

242a **Leaves consisting of a sheath at the base of the slender stem (with or without a continuing tonguelike blade), or with a bladelike involucre at the base of the flower spikelets, the involucre continuing and appearing as an extension of the stem; flowers borne in overlapping scales, consisting of 1 pistil and 1 to 3 stamens (Bulrush). Fig. 132** .... *Scirpus*

Figure 132

Figure 132 *Scirpus* (Cyperaceae) A. *Scirpus validus*, habit, showing swollen stem base; B. *S. americanus*, habit showing triangular stem; C. Nutlet; D. *S. atrovirens*, habit; E. Spikelet; F. Nutlet.

This genus contains both emergent species (sometimes growing in water 3 M in depth) or marginal and shore forms. Included are the common Bulrushes that have many economic importances (boat-building, baskets, mats, *etc.*) *Scirpus validus* grows to a height of 15 or 20 feet. *S. americanus* often forms dense stands on beaches and in shallow water. Species like *S. atrovirens* or *S. atrocinctus* form stands in swales and ditches. *S. subterminalis* grows submersed and forms dense meadows of grasslike plants with the stem and leaves lax and floating. Stems of *Scirpus* are either

triangular or round in cross section. The inflorescence of spikelets is subterminal with subtending involucral leaves (grasslike in *S. atrovirens, e.g.*) which may be round in cross section and extend beyond the inflorescence so as to appear like a continuation of the stem. Species have many biological importances, as food for muskrats, nesting sites for birds, as soilbinders and in the ageing of lakes.

242b Plants otherwise **243**

243a Leaves occurring as basal sheaths which are open, without any tongue-like or bladelike extensions, and with a stemlike extension of the involucre which often appears as an elongation of the stem beyond the cluster of brown flowers, the flowers thus appearing to be lateral near the top of the stem; flowers with 3 sepals and petals, and with 3 or 6 stamens, the flowers appearing as small, brown lilylike blooms; capsule with many seeds (Rush). Fig. 133 ....
.... *Juncus**

(*) *Luzula*, a related genus of semi-aquatic habitats has closed sheaths and a capsulelike fruit which has 3 seeds.

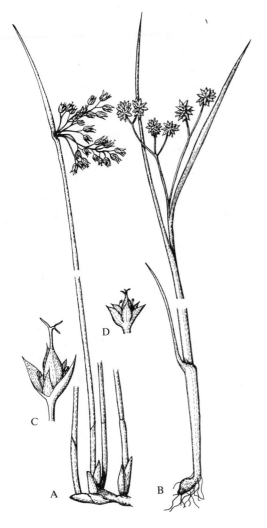

near the tip, and extending from its base a round leaf which appears as a continuation of the stem. The sheath at the base may or may not have a flat blade extending from the margin. The thickened plant bases are used by muskrats for food, and the seeds are used by upland birds.

243b Leaves occurring only as a collarlike sheath at the base of the stem; spikelets terminal on elongate, naked stems which may be angular (*E. Robbinsii*) or round in cross section; pistil with a persistent style which enlarges to form a tubercle at the summit of the nutlet (Spike Rush). Fig. 134 .... *Eleocharis*

Figure 133

Figure 133 *Juncus* (Juncaceae) A. *Juncus effusus*, habit of plant portion; B. *J. nodosus;* C. Flower of *J. effusus;* D. Flower of *J. nodosus.*

Species of this genus are ofter clumped, with several to many culms in each plant. There are two principal expressions; one being a naked stem with a sheath at the base. Another form is a leaf-bearing stem with flat blades. The leafless stems have a cluster of flowers

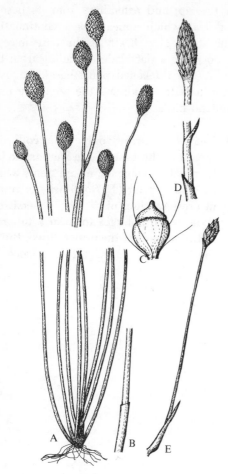

Figure 134

Figure 134 *Eleocharis* (Cyperaceae) A. *Eleocharis obtusa,* habit of plant; B. Sheath at base of culm; C. Nutlet; D. *E. palustris,* lower part of stem and terminal head of flowers; E. *E. albida,* habit of a flowering shoot.

There are many aquatic and semi-aquatic species in this genus, growing submersed, emergent, and marginal. Some are important in succession as ponds age and disappear. The plants are distinctive in having a solitary spike at the apex of a naked culm, hence the name of Spike Rush. Some species are short and form a turf on lake bottoms, in shallow water, or on

muddy shores. Others are tall, clumped and tufted, as much as 4 dm high. These plants are important as soil binders, and as food for birds. Muskrats also are known to use these plants as food.

244a (240) **Leaves basal (or nearly so), sometimes with a few leaves on the stem** 245

244b **Leaves mostly borne on an elongated stem (rarely a few basal leaves also)** ....
.... 269

245a **Leaves with flat blades (at least in part), slender, grasslike or ribbonlike, tapering to a fine point** 246

245b **Leaves round in cross section (or nearly so), slender and threadlike with margins parallel or subparallel** 261

246a **Plants submersed (or incidentally stranded)** 247

246b **Plants emergent or growing on shores and in wet meadows** 252

247a **Leaves long (up to 1 M), flat, ribbonlike** 248

247b **Leaves shorter, not ribbonlike, but grasslike or awllike, tapering to a point** 251

248a **Leaves somewhat rubbery or leathery; vein not showing, or scarcely so; stem branched; leaves often basal but sometimes on the stem also; flowers solitary, arising from a spathe (Mud Plantain). Fig. 94** .... *Heteranthera*

248b Plants otherwise; not branched; leaves mostly basal (sometimes a few on the stem); veins apparent 249

249a Leaves clustered, ribbonlike, up to 3 feet long; all from a subterranean rootstock, showing a prominent midvein (See Fig. 135-d), and several lateral parallel nerves, with a marginal zone in which there are only a few cross veinlets, thus forming a distinct border; flowers of two sorts; pistillate solitary on a long, slender scape, the bloom floating at the surface; staminate flowers on a basal spathe; plants mostly of deep water (**Water Celery**). Fig. 135 .... *Vallisneria*

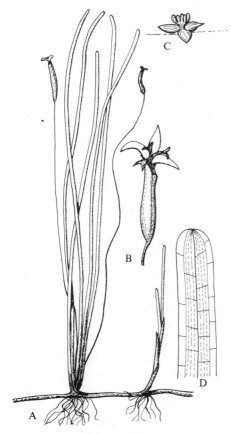

Figure 135

Figure 135 *Vallisneria americana* (Hydrocharitaceae) A. Habit of plant with pistillate flowers; B. Pistillate flower and spathe; C. Staminate flower floating at surface after release from base of plant; D. Leaf tip.

The long, ribbonlike leaves arise vertically, but lax, in tufts from a creeping rootstock. Sometimes the leaves are a full meter in length. Plants may form veritable "forests" in quiet water and provide suitable cover for small fish. Muskrats, fish and birds use *Vallisneria* for food. Pistillate flowers float at the surface on a long, spiral thread from the bottom, whereas staminate flowers are in stalked spathes in the axils of the leaves. These break loose and float to the surface at maturity. *Vallisneria* is often planted in fish nurse ponds (as Water Celery). This is a species which is widely distributed throughout the United States wherever there are suitable habitats. *V. neotropicalis* grows in subtropical United States.

249b Plants otherwise; leaves differently veined 250

250a Leaves clustered, mostly basal, long lax, ribbonlike (often floating at the surface), usually bluntly pointed but acute in some forms, without prominent longitudinal veins, the cross and longitudinal veinlets forming a meshwork of rectangular, cubical spaces; flowers in heads, monoecious, the lower pistillate and the upper staminate, the heads beadlike in arrangement in the upper part of the stem; perianth consisting of scales (**Bur Reed**). Fig. 136 .... *Sparganium*

Figure 136

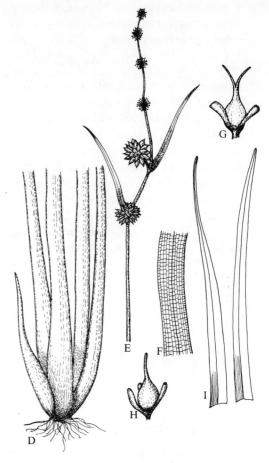

Figure 136 Continued

Figure 136 *Sparganium* (Sparganiaceae) A. *Sparganium chlorocarpum* type habit showing base of leaves and inflorescence at apex of plant; B. Fruit; C. Cross section of leaf (diagram); D. *S. androcladum* type, base of plant; E. Inflorescence; F. Section of leaf to show venation; G. Flower; H. Nutlet; I. Tips of leaves.

Most species are found emergent in lake margins and sloughs, but some (*Sparganium fluctuans*) are submersed in deep ponds, the ribbonlike leaves floating at the surface. Emergent leaves are trough-shaped or keeled on the back in the basal portion. Burlike heads of fruits may be as much as 5 cm in diameter and are used by wildfowl whereas muskrats devour the entire plant.

250b Leaves ribbonlike but very narrow (2 to 10 mm wide); clustered, erect, but lax and often floating at the surface; with one prominent midvein and several, indistinct parallel nerves, the cross veinlets forming a pattern of larger elongate, rectangular spaces; perianth of 3 green sepals and 3 white petals; flowers in whorls on a long, naked scape; some flowers with either stamens or pistils only (Arrowhead; Delta Potato). Fig. 92 .... *Sagittaria*

251a (247) Leaves dark green, stiff, awllike but somewhat flattened, in general filiform, with a broad sheath at the base, blades up to 3 mm wide in the midregion; flowers monoecious, the carpellate in pairs; the staminate solitary on a naked, erect scape. Fig. 137 .... *Littorella*

Figure 137

Figure 137 *Littorella americana* (Plantaginaceae) A. Habit of plant; B. Pistillate flower.

This is a small plant, with leaves up to 7 cm long, growing submersed in northern states. In the vegetative condition it is difficult to differentiate these small plants from *Ruppia* and from *Ranunculus reptans*. Plants are monoecious, the staminate being on a scape whereas the pistillate are at the base of the scape. No biological importance is attached to this species.

251b Leaves not dark green, but awllike, somewhat flattened, up to 3 cm long, not sheathing at the base; inflorescence a scape with a few small, white flowers in a raceme; 4 petals and sepals; plants of shallow water (Awlwort). Fig. 138 .... *Subularia*

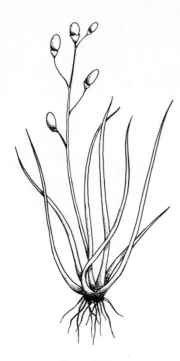

Figure 138

Figure 138   *Subularia aquatica* (Cruciferae)
Habit.

The linear, basal leaves forming a rosette are
much unlike other members of the mustard
family. The flowering scape with white flowers may be as much as 10 cm high. *S. aquatica*
is rare but occurs in both Atlantic and Pacific states. As far as is known *Subularia* has
no biological importances.

**252a (246) Leaves flat, 2-ranked, swordlike,
equitant-sheathing at the base; inflorescence a spadix of numerous, closely arranged flowers composed of 6 yellowish
bracts, 6 stamens and a pistil; the spadix
cylindrical and borne on a scape with
a spathe continuing beyond the spadix
as an extension of the scape; plants spicy
aromatic (Sweet Flag). Fig. 139** ....
.... *Acorus*

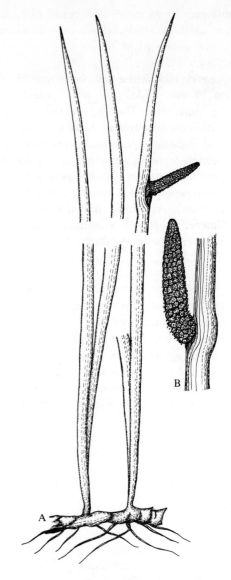

Figure 139

Figure 139   *Acorus calamus* (Araceae) A.
Habit of plant; B. Spadix.

The sheathing, narrow but swordlike leaves
of *Acorus* superficially resemble young *Typha*
plants. They may be as much as one M in
height, growing among cattail in the margins
of lakes and in lagoons and marshes. The thick

rhizomes are much used by muskrats for food. The spicy aroma from crushed leaves explains the common name of Sweet Flag. Records show that *Acorus* is absent from southwest and southeastern United States.

252b Plants otherwise; leaves not equitant ....
.... **253**

253a Leaves grasslike, mostly basal, but some cauline; flowers in spikelets that are closely arranged to form a head or umbel, with one or more leaf-like bracts below the head, the inflorescence a long shoot that is almost naked, sometimes with a few bractlike leaves; bristles of flowers long, becoming white and forming "cotton balls" (Cotton Grass). Fig. 140 .... ***Eriophorum***

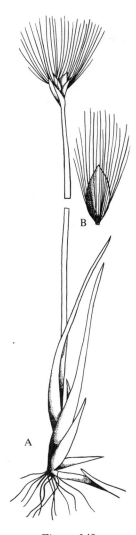

Figure 140

Figure 140 *Eriophorum* (Cyperaceae) A. Habit of plant; B. Scale with bristles.

Species grow mostly in *Sphagnum* bogs where they are showy as Cotton Grass. In the tundras of the Arctic conspicuous white stands are produced. The "cotton" appearance is a result of the long, fine bristles of the inflorescence scales, the spikelets forming a dense terminal head. It is not known that *Eriophorum* has any biological importances.

253b Plants otherwise; inflorescence not forming a cotton ball 254

254a Plants with a stout rhizome, giving rise to long, slender scapes bearing spikelets of flowers subterminally, and with a tuft of long slender leaves at the base; plants submersed (Bulrush). Fig. 141 ....
.... *Scirpus subterminalis*

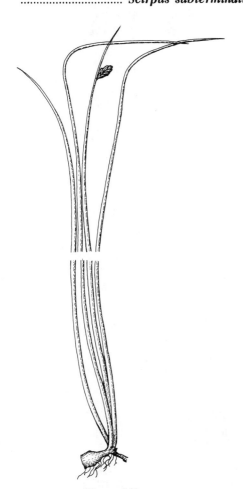

Figure 141

Figure 141 *Scirpus subterminalis* (Cyperaceae) Habit of plant.

This species has long, lax leaves from the base, the plant growing submersed and often forming dense "meadows." The leaves and the flowering stem float at the surface of the water. The inflorescence has but one spikelet. The species is important in both fishery and aquatic bird biology.

254b Plants otherwise **255**

255a Leaves grasslike, sometimes broad and inflated, sheathed for as much as one-half their length; inflorescence a long, slender scape with a round head of imbricated scales, yellowish flowers in their axils (Yellow-eyed Grass). Fig. 142 .... *Xyris*

Figure 142

Figure 142 *Xyris torta* (Xyridaceae) Habit.

The Yellow-eyed Grasses grow on beaches or in wet meadows, and occasionally in water at lake margins. In general they may be used as an index of acid situations. The long, narrow leaves are flat and are sheathed for as much as one-half their length. The small flowers occur in globular or oval heads at the end of naked scapes and are in the axils of bracts. It is claimed that mallard ducks use *Xyris* for food.

255b Leaves not sheathed as above; inflorescence not a head on naked scape 256

256a Leaves with a broad, membranous sheath that bears a pair of ligulelike lobes at the upper margin; inflorescence a long, slender spike with numerous, small 3-merous flowers (Arrow Grass). Fig. 143 .... *Triglochin*

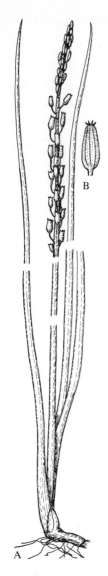

be no biological importance. There are 3 widely distributed species in the United States.

256b Leaves without a basal sheath that bears ligules **257**

257a Leaves sheathing at the base, from a slender rootstock; inflorescence a head or short raceme on a long, slender, naked scape that is dotted with sticky glands (False Asphodel). Fig. 144 .... *Tofieldia*

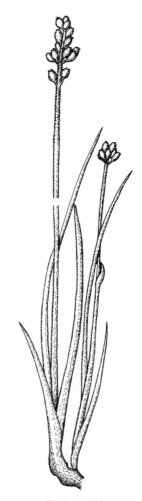

Figure 143

Figure 143 *Triglochin maritima* (Juncaginaceae) A. Habit of plant; B. Capsule.

This genus occurs as a clump of long, slender, basal leaves and a spike of small, green, lily-like flowers. *T. maritima* is the most common species of the genus, occurring in salt and alkaline marshes or basic soils. There appears to

Figure 144

Figure 144   *Tofieldia glutinosa* (Liliaceae) Habit of plant.

This is an herb with 3-parted, yellow flowers, many in a head at the apex of a naked scape. The leaves are elongate-linear and remindful of *Triglochin*. The species is found in bogs and wet meadows, especially at higher altitudes.

257b Plants otherwise; without sticky glands on the flowering scape 258

258a Leaves long and slender, more or less erect, up to 1 M long; flowers showy, blue or pink, in an umbel (Flowering Rush). Fig. 145 .... *Butomus*

Figure 145

Figure 145   *Butomus umbellatus* (Butomaceae) Habit of plant.

This is a tall, showy plant with a naked scape bearing an umbel of blue flowers (or pinkish). There is a tuft of linear, basal leaves nearly as long as the flowering shoot which may be 1 M tall. The leaves are sheathing and keeled in the basal section. *Butomus* is limited in distribution to northern United States, but has been transplanted to various parts of the country by sportsmen clubs since it is useful as wildfowl food.

258b Leaves shorter; inflorescence otherwise **259**

259a Leaves up to 10 cm long, broad at the base from a padlike stem, rather rigid; inflorescence a compact head, the intervening bracts white-tipped and giving a woolly appearance; roots white and showing septations (Pipewort). Fig. 146 .... *Eriocaulon*

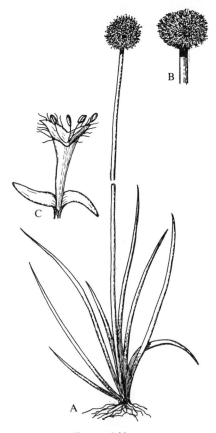

Figure 146

Figure 146 *Eriocaulon septangulare* (Eriocaulaceae) A. Habit of plant; B. Head of flowers; C. Single flower.

There are several species of *Eriocaulon* which are limited in their distribution. They occur as linear-leaved, tufted plants. The elongate leaves are either flat or concave, shorter than the long, naked scape which bears a spherical head of small flowers that are whitish and woolly. Plants are indices of sandy, acid soil and are commonly found in marshes and on grassy beaches, *E. septangulare* is widely distributed in midwest and northern United States.

259b Leaves mostly shorter; inflorescence otherwise **260**

260a Plants essentially without a stem; leaves clustered, broad at the base and imbricate, often awl-shaped but sometimes flattened; flowers small, white, 2 or 3 in a raceme that usually exceeds the length of the leaves (Awlwort). Fig. 138 .... *Subularia*

260b Plants with creeping stems; leaves tufted but filiform throughout their length, not imbricate at the base; flowers small (3 mm wide), white or purple, solitary on a slender, naked, recurved stalk; flowers 5-parted (Mudwort). Fig. 98 .... *Limosella*

261a (245) Leaves hollow and tubular, in a rosette from a padlike stem, broadened at the base to enclose a sporangium; the stem bearing a mass of short roots (Quillwort Fern). Fig. 147 .... *Isoetes*

Figure 147

Figure 147 *Isoetes* (Isoetaceae) A. Habit of plant; B. Base of leaf showing sporangium.

This fern appears as a clump of bunchgrass, either submersed or in wet meadows. Some species have leaves nearly 1 M tall. The hollow leaves from a padlike stem have a sporangium at the base on the inner (adaxial) face when mature. Some species constitute an index for soft-water or acid habitats where they sometimes form a veritable meadows over lake bottoms. The plants are used as food by some diving birds, by deer and by muskrats.

261b Leaves not hollow; not bearing sporangia **262**

262a Plants dwarfed (3 to 6 cm tall, rarely up to 10 cm), prostrate with creeping stem, sometimes a threadlike rootstocks from which tufted leaves arise 263

262b Plants larger, leaves up to 6 dm tall; flowering scapes up to 12 dm tall; with thick rootstocks, or pads; leaves mostly in rosettes 266

263a Leaves slender, 2 to 4 cm long (up to 5 cm), in clumps of 2 or 3 (sometimes only 1) from each node of a prostrate, threadlike stem; plants forming dense mats (submersed or on shores); flowers yellow, solitary at the nodes (Buttercup; Water Spearwort). Fig. 148 .... *Ranunculus reptans*

Figure 148

Figure 148 *Ranunculus reptans* (Ranunculaceae) Habit of plant.

This species of water buttercup is unlike others in the genus in having tufted, linear or spatulate leaves on creeping stems. From the nodes solitary flowers on relatively long peduncles arise. This species is found on muddy shores.

263b Plants otherwise, mostly larger; leaves 6 cm tall, rarely up to 10 cm 264

264a Leaves dark green, rather stiff, filiform (but somewhat flattened), up to 3 mm wide in the midregion, with a broad sheathed base; flowers on a slender, erect scape, monoecious, the carpellate in pairs, the staminate solitary. Fig. 137 .... *Littorella*

264b Plants otherwise; leaves without a broad sheath at the base 265

265a Leaves mostly basal but sometimes alternate on the stem; stipules fused at base of leaves; flowers minute, in an umbel on a scape that is borne on an erect shoot and sheathed by a leaf base; flowers simple, consisting of 2 sessile stamens and 4 sessile pistils (Widgeon Grass). Fig. 149 .... *Ruppia*

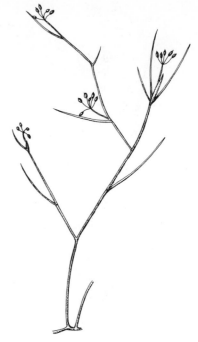

Figure 149

Figure 149 *Ruppia maritima* (Ruppiaceae) Habit of plant.

This plant has slender, grasslike leaves which are broader at the base and sheathing, arising from prostrate runners. A short or long flowering scape arises from the same node as the leaves. *Ruppia* is found throughout the United States on saline or alkaline shores. The fruits are much used by aquatic birds.

265b Leaves in tufts of from 5 to 10 on threadlike runners; flowers perfect, 3 mm wide, white or purple, solitary on a recurved peduncle from the stem node (Mudwort). Fig. 98 .... *Limosella*

266a (262) Plants with long, terete leaves, up to 6 dm tall; scapes 12 dm, sheathed at the base and arising from a short rhizome which is covered with white

leaf bases of old leaves, the sheath with a ligule; inflorescence a crowded, spike-like raceme (Arrow Grass). Fig. 143 ....
.... *Triglochin*

266b Plants smaller; inflorescence not a spike
.... 267

267a Plants stemless; leaves short, 3 cm tall, awllike, in a tuft; inflorescence a scape with a few small, white flowers in a raceme; several scapes arising from each leaf tuft; flowers with 4 petals and sepals (Awlwort). Fig. 138 .... *Subularia*

267b Plants otherwise; leaves longer 268

268a Plants with leaves to 60 cm (usually about 35 cm), not translucent; sheathing for as much as one-half their length; inflorescence an ovate spike, with perfect and imperfect flowers intermixed, consisting of a sessile stamen and a single carpel, or at times with 2 basal pistillate flowers in leaf axes (Flowering Quillwort). Fig. 150 .... *Lilaea*

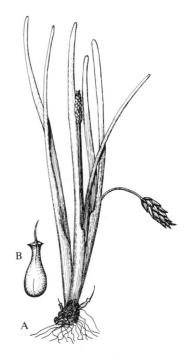

Figure 150

Figure 150 *Lilaea subulata* (Juncaginaceae) A. Habit; B. Basal achene (stylized).

This species has linear, ribbonlike leaves, sheathing at the base, which may be up to 60 cm tall. Each plant has several naked stalks bearing a cone-shaped spike of flowers. Also some flowers are borne low in the axils of the leaves. *L. subulata* is found on alkaline flats, tidal basins and on deltas of rivers. No biological importance is known.

268b Plant with leaves 2 to 8 cm long, in a basal rosette, translucent when held to the light and showing cross markings; roots white with cross markings; inflorescence a naked stalk, bearing a head of white flowers and bracts which are intermingled, the bracts whitish so that a white head is produced; flowers either pistillate or staminate (Pipewort). Fig. 146 .... *Eriocaulon*

269a (244) Leaves opposite 270

269b Leaves alternate or whorled 278

270a Leaves threadlike, if flat, very narrow with parallel margins, rounded or pointed at the apex 271

270b Leaves elongate, lanceolate or elongate-elliptic, sometimes fleshy 274

271a Leaves filiform and tapering to a point 272

271b Leaves flat, rounded at the apex 273

272a Leaves abruptly broadened at the base, margins with various forms of sharp serrations; leaves linear, up to 8 times the diameter in length, mostly crowded, bunched or whorled, sometimes opposite; flowers solitary in the axils of the leaves (Bushy Pondweed). Fig. 151 .... *Najas*

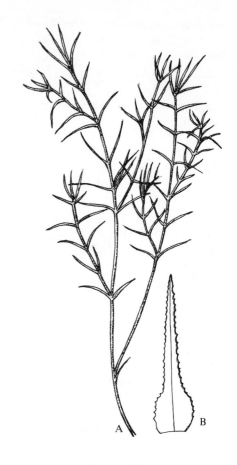

Figure 151

Figure 151 *Najas flexilis* (Najdaceae) A. Habit; B. Leaf showing characteristic base.

This genus is entirely aquatic and submersed, forming bushy growths which may be scattered or in extensive patches. The leaves are linear and have specifically characteristic toothed margins and base shapes. *N. flexilis* is the most common and widely distributed species. It is excellent as an aerator, and the seeds, although scant, are much used by birds for food.

272b Leaves threadlike, filiform, narrowed symmetrically from the base to a fine point, 0.5 mm wide, no serrations on the margins; (leaves sometimes whorled as well as opposite); flowers 2 to 5 in the axils of leaves; plants perennial with a slender rhizome (Horned Pondweed). Fig. 152 .... *Zannichellia*

genus the sessile, monoecious flowers and fruits are borne in the axils of leaves. The flowers, without a calyx or corolla, are borne in a transparent spathe. The fruits are characteristic, being an elongate nutlet with a toothed, longitudinal ridge and an apical beak. *Z. palustris* is widely distributed over the United States in hard water and saline situations. Both the plants and the fruits are used by many birds for food.

273a (271) Leaves narrow ribbons, indented at the apex, margins parallel (becoming spatulate to obovate in the upper part of the stem), forming a rosette at the apex of the stem; plants monoecious, stems unbranched (Water Starwort). Fig. 47 .... *Callitriche*

273b Leaves narrow and not widened at the base, the same shape throughout the length of the stem; flowers perfect; stems branched (Water Purslane). Fig. 153 .... *Didiplis*

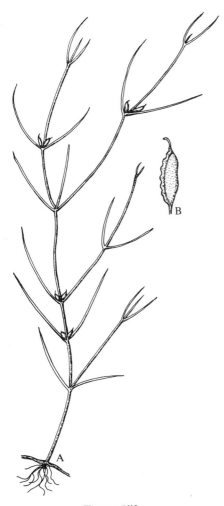

Figure 152

Figure 152 *Zannichellia palustris* (Zanichellaceae) A. Habit; B. Fruit.

Leaves are linear and opposite and rather sparse as compared with *Naias*. Like that

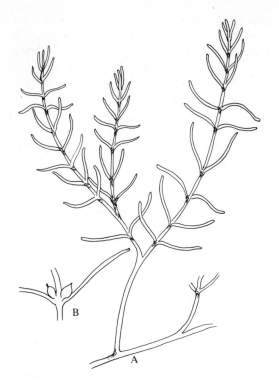

Figure 153

Figure 153 *Didiplis* (Lythraceae) A. Habit of *Didiplis linearis;* B. Location of fruits.

Some species of *Didiplis* are strictly aquatic (*D. linearis, D. diandra*), or they may occur in the shallow water of lakes and continuing onto the shore mud. They are found mostly in eastern United States. The plants are dwarfish; have narrow, opposite leaves, although some varieties of the species have elongate-oval leaves (*D. diandra* especially). The flowers are small, greenish and are borne in the axils of the leaves. *Peplis diandra* is a synonym of the latter species name.

274a (270) Leaves elongate-ellipsoid, long-tapering at the base; flowers purple, in a dense cluster on a stalk arising in the axils of the leaves (Water Willow). Fig. 55 .... *Dianthera* (*Justicia*)

274b Plants otherwise 275

275a Leaves thin, oblong to linear, without a long-tapering base; flowers solitary, sessile or nearly so in the axils of leaves (Sea Milkwort). Fig. 25 .... *Glaux*

275b Plants otherwise 276

276a Leaves oblong-lanceolate, broad at the base and lobed, tapering to a sharp point; flowers sessile or on very short stalks. Fig. 154 .... *Ammannia*

Figure 154

Figure 154 *Ammania auriculata* (Lythraceae) A. Habit; B. Fruits.

The clasping leaves of this species are lanceolate, with one or two flowers in the axils. The plants are erect, growing on lake margins and in marshes. The stems are square in cross section. There are three semi-aquatic species in the genus, distributed in eastern and southern United States, *A. auriculata* being the most common.

276b Plants otherwise **277**

277a Leaves linear, fleshy or succulent, with scalelike stipules, nearly round in cross section; leaves often fascicled although sometimes opposite; flowers pink or white, in terminal racemes (Sand Spurry). Fig. 155 .... *Spergularia*

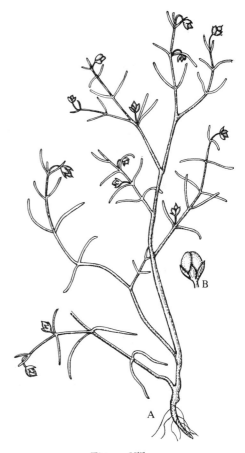

Figure 155

Figure 155 *Spergularia canadensis* (Caryophyllaceae) A. Habit; B. Capsule.

This plant sprawls on tidal flats and on saline beaches. They are relatively small; have linear, opposite leaves which are nearly round in cross section. The small 5-merous flowers are solitary in the axils of leaves. This species occurs on both Atlantic and Pacific coasts in northern sections.

277b Leaves not fleshy, narrow but flat, elongate-elliptic with narrowed bases and a short petiole; flowers solitary in the axils of leaves (Tooth-cup). Fig. 54 .... *Rotala*

278a (269) Leaves whorled or bunched .. 279

278b Leaves alternate **281**

279a Leaves grasslike, mostly alternate, but the involucral leaves sometimes whorled (Sedge). Fig. 156 .... *Cyperus*

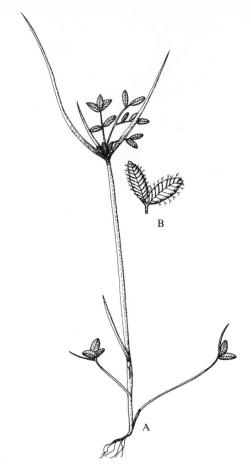

Figure 156

Figure 156 *Cyperus* sp. (Cyperaceae) A. Habit; B. Spikelet.

This is a sedge with a solid, angular stem (in cross section) that has an inflorescence in which the scales are arranged in two rows. The spikelet of flowers accordingly is flattened, giving species in this genus a distinct appearance when in flower. *C. esculenta* (chufa) is a common beach species on which root tubers are formed (Ground Almonds) that are much-used by aquatic birds for food. Some species grow in shallow water, but mostly these are plants of grassy margins, wet meadows and ditches.

279b Leaves not grasslike in shape **280**

280a Plants bushy with branched stems; leaves tufted or whorled, filiform with an abruptly widened base, the margins toothed; (leaves occasionally opposite) (Bushy Pondweed). Fig. 151 ...... *Najus*

280b Plants without leaves tufted but in distinct whorls, as many as 12 at the node of an unbranched stem; submersed leaves longer (12 times longer than wide) and more lax than the leaves on the emergent section of the stem; flowers solitary, sessile, in the axils of leaves (Water Mare's Trail). Fig. 41 ....
.... *Hippuris*

281a (278) Leaves swordlike, sheathing blades, equitant, partly or mostly basal, from a thick rootstock (Flag). Fig. 157
.... *Iris*

Figure 157

Figure 157 *Iris* (Iridaceae) A. Habit; B. Capsule.

The flag with its flat, sheathing swordlike leaves is clearly recognized, even when not in bloom. At least seven species occur in marshes and swamps. The most common is *I. versicolor* with blue flowers. *I. fulva* and *I. pseudacorus* are yellow or copper-colored. Muskrats are known to use the rootstocks for food.

281b Leaves not flat and swordlike, and not equitant **282**

282a Leaves filiform, dichotomously forked (Riverweed). Fig. 107 .... *Podostemum*

282b Plants otherwise 283

283a Leaves short-filiform, not divided, simple, mostly basal but a few alternate on the stem, occurring in tufts from a horizontal runner; flowers in a simple umbel on a long or short stalk (Widgeon Grass). Fig. 149 .... *Ruppia*

283b Plants otherwise 284

284a Plants with long-filiform leaves, thread-like from 0.1 to 3.0 mm wide, leaves with stipules (Pondweed). Fig. 46 .... *Potamogeton*

284b Plants otherwise 285

285a Leaves long (1/2 to 2 M) and ribbon-like, flat or keeled at the back, the margins parallel; leaves lax when in water, or relatively rigid and erect when emergent 286

285b Leaves shorter, up to 1 1/2 dm long, grasslike or linear, tapering gradually to a point 289

286a Plants of marine and brackish waters 287

286b Plants of fresh water or terrestrial .. 288

287a Leaves up to 2 M long, slender, up to 6 mm wide, somewhat flattened to nearly terete, the leaf tip truncate or notched, the leaves arising from a stout, much-branched rhizome and sheathed at the base; flowers in a spadix which is enclosed by a spathe, the flowers in 2 rows on one side of the spike; carpellate flower with an obovate or cordate pistil, a short style and divergent stigma; plants dioecious (Surf Grass). Fig. 158 .... *Phyllospadix*

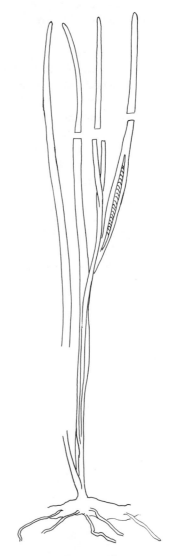

Figure 158

Figure 158 *Phyllospadix scouleri* (Potamogetonaceae) Habit of plant.

There are two species of this genus in the shore waters of the Pacific. They are found in tide pools or on wave-swept rocks. The plants are similar to *Zostera* but differ in being dioecious and having a different type of rhizome. The plants are important as substrates for algae and small animals in marine biology.

287b **Leaves up to 1 1/2 M long, wider than above (up to 12 mm at the base), rising from a slender rootstock, bluntly rounded at the apex; erect stem leafy; plants monoecious; inflorescence a spadix, with two sorts of flowers alternate in 2 rows along the axis; the carpellate flowers with a broadly ovoid ovary that has a long style and an erect stigma (Eel Grass). Fig. 159 .... *Zostera***

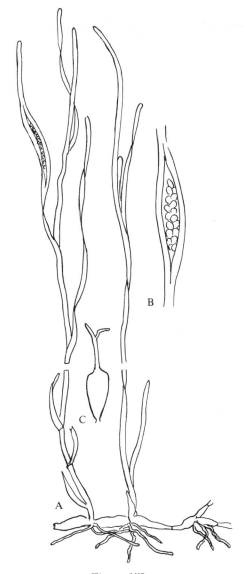

Figure 159

Figure 159 *Zostera marina* (Potamogetonaceae) A. Habit of basal and apical portions of plant; B. Spadix; C. Carpel.

This is the widely distributed and familiar Eel Grass, abundant in certain sections all along both the Pacific and Atlantic coasts of the United States, usually growing in quiet, back waters and on muddy bottoms. The long, ribbonlike leaves are used as food by many animals and plants serve as substrate for marine algae, Bryozoa, etc.

288a Plants rank, tall stem (up to 2 1/2 M), with long (about 1 M) leaves, up to 20 mm wide, sheathing at the base, the sheath abruptly narrowed at the blade base, bluntly pointed at the apex; inflorescence a double spike composed of numerous staminate flowers above, the pistillate flowers compactly arranged to form a firm cylinder below; plants of shores or emergent in shallow water (not submersed) (Cattail). Fig. 160 .... *Typha*

Figure 160 *Typha* (Typhaeceae) A. *Typha latifolia,* upper portion of leaves and flowering spike; B. Pollen grains; C. *Typha angustifolia,* upper portion of plant showing staminate and pistillate spikes separated; D. Pollen; E. Base of plant; F. Leaf tip.

The familiar cattail is widely distributed over the world, occurring as several species. *T. latifolia* is the most common in this country. It has relatively wide leaves and the terminal staminate spike is in contact with the lower pistillate spike; has multicellular pollen grains. In *T. angustifolia* the leaves are very narrow ribbons; the spikes of flowers are smaller and there is a sterile section of stem appearing between the staminate and pistillate columns. The pollen grains are one-celled. Dense *Typha* stands provide excellent cover for birds and other animals. The rhizomes are used by muskrats and beavers, and land mammals sometimes browse on the shoots. Young sprouts and inner parts of the shoots can be used for human food.

288b Plants shorter, erect and emergent or submersed with long, (up to 2 M) flexible, ribbonlike leaves, emergent leaves up to 4 dm long and erect, flat above but keeled on the back below; the leaves sheathing at the base and with a few alternate on the stem, the sheath gradually narrowed at the blade base (Bur Reed). Fig. 136 .... *Sparganium*

289a (285) Leaves linear, fleshy and terete or nearly so, relatively short, up to 4 cm long; flowers sometimes solitary but usually several clustered in the axils of leaves; plants stout or somewhat shrubby (Sea Blite). Fig. 161 .... *Suaeda*

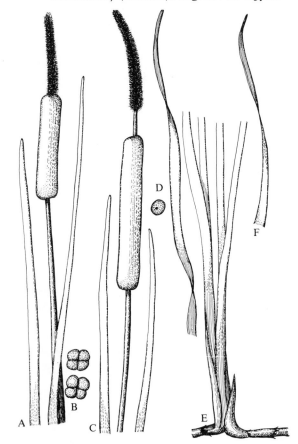

Figure 160

Figure 161

Figure 161 *Suaeda* (Chenopodiaceae) A.
Habit of *S. torreyana*; B. *S. linearis*, single
flower; C. Section of stem.

Like so many brackish water and saline plants,
the leaves are narrow, fleshy and nearly
round. The flowers are solitary or several together in the axils of leaves. There are three

species along the coasts of the United States,
Suaeda maritima occurring on both Atlantic
and Pacific shores. *S. depressa* and *S. Torreyana* occur in saline or brackish soils inland.

289b Leaves longer, grasslike, broad at the
base and tapering to a point, flat, not
terete and fleshy 290

290a Plants submersed; stems lax and drifting but rooted; leaves with parallel
veins 291

290b Plants otherwise 292

291a Plants with thin leaves that have parallel veins or nerves, and with stipules
which are either free or clasping; plants
often with broad, floating leaves and
in a few species the submersed leaves
reduced to quills (Pondweed). Fig. 46
.... *Potamogeton*

291b Plants with thick, sometimes rubbery
leaves (often ribbonlike but sometimes
grasslike), gradually tapering to a point,
without a distinct midrib; stipules lacking; floating leaves wanting (Mud
Plantain). Fig. 94 .... *Heteranthera*

292a (290) *The following genera must be
differentiated by type of inflorescence
and by characteristics of flower and
fruit. Vegetatively they are very similar,
with slender, naked stems, or with grasslike, mostly alternate leaves.*

Inflorescence a close cluster of brown flowers appearing to be lateral on an elongated, naked stem, or a cymelike open panicle terminating the stem; flowers composed of 3 brown sepals and petals, 3 or 6 stamens and a superior pistil; leaves slender, alternate on the stem, or as blades arising from a basal sheath (Rush). Fig. 133 .... *Juncus*

292b Inflorescence various, a headlike cluster or compound raceme, or a simple one, usually with one or more involucral, grasslike leaves; the inflorescence composed of overlapping bracts with florets in the axils, the flower composed of several bristles (or as an inner scale) as a perianth which is sometimes reduced or lacking, with 1 to 3 stamens and 1 pistil bearing a characteristic style according to the genus 293

293a All flowers imperfect, the staminate and pistillate in the same cluster (spike) or in separate spikes on the same plant; the pistil enclosed by a membranous sac (perigynium) (Sedge). Fig. 162 .... *Carex*

Figure 162   *Carex* (Cyperaceae) A. *Carex stipata*, habit; B. Perigynium; C. Scale; D. Tip of sheath; E. *C. bebbii*, habit of plant at tip; F. *C. lasiocarpa*, tip of plant; G. Rolled leaf; H. Perigynium; I. *C. comosa*, perigynium and scale; J. *C. tuckermannii*, perigynium and scale; K. *C. bullata perigynium* and scale; L. *C. rostrata*, base of plant; M. Tip of plant; N. Perigynium; O. Scale; P. *C. pseudocyperus*, tip of plant; Q. Perigynium; R. Scale.

Species of *Carex* are solitary or clumped. There are two chief expressions, one in which there are two kinds of flowers intermixed in a terminal spike, and a group in which the staminate spikes (above) are separate from the pistillate spikes (below). The genus is peculiar in having the ovary inclosed in a variously shaped sac called the perigynium. The many species are marginal, occurring in marshes and wet meadows, and along shores. *C. lasiocarpa* is an important builder of soil in bogs and bays, speeding the ageing of lakes.

293b Flowers all perfect, or sometimes with perfect flowers and some with stamens only in the same spike 294

294a Inflorescence a single spikelet, terminal on a long, naked stem 295

294b Inflorescence not as above 297

295a Spikelet terminal oval, elliptic or nearly round, with flower bristles inconspicuous or absent; culms angular or round in cross section (Spike Rush). Fig. 134 .... *Eleocharis*

295b Bristles conspicuous, long and silky, often white or tawny 296

296a Bristles numerous, silky and white (becoming tawny), smooth (Cotton Grass). Fig. 140 .... *Eriophorum*

Figure 162

Figure 162 Continued

296b Bristles at the base of the nutlet few (1 to 8), or none, barbed (rarely smooth in some species), white and silky, nutlets (achenes) elongate (Alpine Cotton Grass). Fig. 163 .... *Scirpus hudsonianus*

Figure 163

Figure 163 *Scirpus hudsonianus* (Cyperaceae) A. Habit; B. Nutlet and bristles.

This species resembles *Eriophorum* and at times has been classified there. The bristles are relatively few in number (about 4) and are toothed. Plants are well-named Cotton Grass; occur in *Sphagnum* bogs and wet meadows.

297a (294) Stems solid, triangular in cross section (sometimes with rounded angles) 298

297b Stems hollow, round in cross section, often leafy with grasslike leaves arising on 3 sides of the stem, one at each node; inflorescence terminal and also axilary (Three-way-Sedge). Fig. 164 .... *Dulichium*

Figure 164

Figure 164 *Dulichium arundinaceum* (Cyperaceae) Habit of plant tip.

This sedge has a hollow stem that is practically round in cross section and one which bears a short, grasslike leaf at almost every node. Flowers arise in a terminal raceme as well as in smaller, axillary racemes. Plants are important as beach-builders; are used sparsely by birds and muskrats.

298a Scales of the spikelet borne in 2 distinct rows, the spikelet accordingly flattened (Sedge). Fig. 156 .... *Cyperus*

298b Scales of the spikelet arising from all sides of the axis, the spikelet in general rounded in cross section 299

299a Spikelets many-flowered 300

299b Spikelet with only 1 or 2 flowers, with several of the lower scales sterile 301

300a Leaf above the spikelets round in cross section, appearing as a continuation of the stem; achene lacking a tubercle; lowermost scales of the spikelet only sterile (Bulrush). Fig. 132 .... *Scirpus americanus*

300b Leaf or leaves above the spikelets not round in cross section, but grasslike, with blades tapering to a point; leaves below the spikelets sometimes appearing to be whorled (Bulrush). Fig. 132 c, d .... *Scirpus* spp.

301a Achenes lacking a tubercle and with no basal bristles about the achene (Twig Rush). Fig. 165 .... *Cladium*

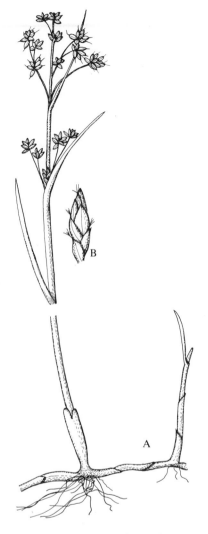

Figure 165

301b Achene with a prominent tubercle of various forms, subtended by bristles; spikelets with empty scales below the fertile ones, the spikelets often densely clustered to form heads (Beak Rush). Fig. 166 .... *Rynchospora*

Figure 166

Figure 165 *Cladium* (Cyperaceae) A. *Cladium mariscoides,* habit of plant; B. spikelet.

This plant has cylindrical spikelets with only the uppermost bearing flowers. Stems are usually leafy and may be as much as 1 M tall. They bear a much-branched inflorescence with several spikelets on each branch. *C. mariscoides* is the most common species throughout most of the eastern half of the United States. There is no known biological importance.

Figure 166 *Rynchospora* (Cyperaceae) A. *Rynchospora alba,* habit of upper portion of stem; B. Nutlet; C. *R. macrostachya,* habit of stem tip; D. Nutlet.

The Beak Rush is well-named because the nutlet bears a prominent tubercle. The spikelet cluster has several leafy involucres which appear as a whorl. *R. macrostachya* is a common member of a *Sphagnum* bog flora, usually standing above the other vegetation and showing the spikelets in dense clumps. The tubercles may be as much as 2.2 cm long.

Check List of Aquatic Plant Genera and Their Family Classification[*][**]

(For reference the family names are arranged alphabetically within their respective major plant groups.)
(*) Generic names marked with * are not included in the Key.
(**) Family names marked with ! are strictly aquatic. The family may include 1 or more species growing in mud.

RHODOPHYTA

Batrachospermaceae !
Batrachospermum
Fig. 12, pp. 19, 20

CHLOROPHYTA

Characeae !
Chara
Fig. 9, p. 17
Nitella
Fig. 10, p. 18
Tolypella
Fig. 11, p. 19
Cladophoraceae !
Cladophora
Fig. 13, p. 20

BRYOPHYTA

Hepaticae

Harpanthaceae
Chiloscyphus
Fig. 15, p. 21
Marchantiaceae
Conocephalum
Fig. 2, p. 13
Marchantia
Fig. 1, p. 12
Ricciaceae
Riccia
Fig. 7, p. 15
Ricciocarpus
Fig. 8, p. 15

MUSCI

Bartramiaceae
Philonotis *
Fissidentaceae
Fissidens
Fig. 17, p. 22
Fontinalaceae
Fontinalis
Fig. 16, p. 22
Hypnaceae
Drepanocladus
Fig. 18, p. 23
Sphagnaceae
Sphagnum
Fig. 14, p. 21

PTERIDOPHYTA

Equisetaceae
Equisetum
Fig. 123, p. 106
Isoetaceae
Isoetes
Fig. 147, p. 127
Marsileaceae !
Marsilea
Fig. 106, p. 90
Osmundaceae
Osmunda
Fig. 104, p. 89
Parkeriaceae
Ceratopteris
Fig. 87, p. 76
Polypodiaceae
Onoclea *
Salviniaceae !
Azolla
Fig. 19, p. 23
Salvinia
Fig. 20, p. 24

SPERMATOPHYTA

Gymnospermae

Pinaceae
Larix
Fig. 21, p. 24
Picea *
Taxodiaceae
Taxodium
Fig. 22, p. 25

ANGIOSPERMAE

Monocotyledonae

Alismaceae !
Alisma
Fig. 102, p. 87
Damasonium
Fig. 101, p. 87
Echinodorus
Fig. 96, p. 83
Lophotocarpus
Fig. 93, pp. 80, 81
Sagittaris
Fig. 92, pp. 79, 80
Araceae
Acorus
Fig. 139, p. 120
Calla
Fig. 69, p. 61
Lysichitum
Fig. 100, p. 86
Orontium
Fig. 103, p. 88
Peltandra
Fig. 91, p. 79
Pistia
Fig. 86, p. 76

Symplocarpus
Fig. 99, p. 85
Butomaceae
Butomus
Fig. 145, p. 125
Cyperaceae
Carex
Fig. 162, pp. 140-142
Cladium
Fig. 165, p. 145
Cyperus
Fig. 156, p. 134
Dulichium
Fig. 164, p. 144
Eleocharis
Fig. 134, pp. 115, 116
Eriophorum
Fig. 140, p. 121
Rhynchospora
Fig. 166, p. 145
Scirpus
Fig. 132, p. 114
Fig. 141, p. 122
Fig. 163, p. 143
Eriocaulaceae
Eriocaulon
Fig. 146, p. 126
Gramineae
Alopecurus
Fig. 128, p. 110
Beckmannia
Fig. 130, p. 112
Glyceria
Fig. 127, p. 109
Leersia
Fig. 129, p. 111
Phalaris
Fig. 126, p. 109
Phragmites
Fig. 125, p. 108
Spartina
Fig. 131, pp. 112, 113
Zizania
Fig. 124, p. 107
Hydrocharitaceae !
Elodea
Fig. 40, p. 37
Halophila *
Hydrilla
Fig. 40E, p. 37
Limnobium
Fig. 88, p. 77
Thalassia *
Vallisneria
Fig. 135, p. 117
Iridaceae
Iris
Fig. 157, p. 135
Juncaceae
Juncus
Fig. 113, p. 115
Jungaginaceae
Lilaea
Fig. 150, p. 129
Triglochin
Fig. 143, p. 124
Lemnaceae !
Lemna
Fig. 4, p. 14
Spirodela
Fig. 3, p. 13
Wolffia
Fig. 6, p. 15
Wolffiella
Fig. 5, p. 14

Liliaceae
Tofieldia
Fig. 144, pp. 124, 125
Mayacaceae !
Mayaca
Fig. 122, p. 105
Najadaceae !
Najas
Fig. 151, p. 130
Pontederiaceae !
Eichhornia
Fig. 89, p. 77
Heteranthera
Fig. 94, p. 81
Pontederia
Fig. 95, p. 82
Potamogetonaceae !
Potamogeton
Fig. 46, pp. 43, 44
Fig. 56, p. 52
Phyllospadix
Fig. 158, pp. 136, 137
Zostera
Fig. 159, p. 137
Ruppiaceae !
Ruppia
Fig. 149, p. 128
Sparganiaceae !
Sparganium
Fig. 136, p. 118
Typhaceae !
Typha
Fig. 160, p. 138
Xyridaceae
Xyris
Fig. 142, p. 123
Zanichelliaceae !
Zanichellia
Fig. 152, p. 131

DICOTYLEDONAE

Acanthaceae
Dianthera
Fig. 35, p. 51
Amaranthaceae
Acnida
Fig. 85, p. 74
Alternanthera
Fig. 49, pp. 46, 47
Betulaceae
Alnus
Fig. 26, p. 27
Betula *
Borangiaceae
Myosotis
Fig. 82, p. 71
Callitrichaceae
Callitriche
Fig. 47, p. 45
Caryophyllaceae
Spergularia
Fig. 155, p. 133
Ceratophyllaceae !
Ceratophyllum
Fig. 119, p. 102
Chenopodiaceae
Salicornia
Fig. 120, p. 104

Sueda
Fig. 161, p. 139
Compositae
Bidens
Fig. 118, p. 101
Megalodonta
Fig. 63, p. 57
Cornaceae
Cornus
Fig. 28, p. 29
Crassulaceae
Tillaea
Fig. 52, p. 48, 49
Cruciferae
Cardamine
Fig. 74, p. 65
Nasturtium
Fig. 75, p. 66
Neobeckia
Fig. 73, p. 64
Rorippa
Fig. 72, pp. 63, 64
Subularia
Fig. 138, p. 120
Droseraceae
Drosera
Fig. 90, p. 78
Elatinaceae !
Elatine
Fig. 53, p. 49
Ericaceae
Andromeda *
Chamaedaphne
Fig. 30, p. 30
Kalmia
Fig. 27A, p. 28
Ledum *
Vaccinium
Fig. 23, p. 25
Gentianaceae,
Haloragaceae !
Hippuris
Fig. 41, p. 38
Myriophyllum
Fig. 117, p. 99
Fig. 121, p. 104
Proserpinaca
Fig. 77, p. 67
Hydrophyllaceae
Hydrolea
Fig. 84, p. 73
Hypericaceae
Hypericum
Fig. 48, p. 46
Labiatae
Lycopus
Fig. 67, p. 59
Mentha
Fig. 66, p. 59
Physostegia
Fig. 62, p. 56, 57
Scutellaria
Fig. 61, p. 56
Stachys
Fig. 65, p. 58
Lentibulariaceae ! (mostly)
Utricularia
Fig. 116, p. 98
Lobeliaceae
Lobelia
Fig. 81, p. 70

Lythraceae
  Ammannia
    Fig. 154, p. 133
  Decodon
    Fig. 24, p. 26
  Didiplis
    Fig. 153, p. 132
  Lythrum
    Fig. 45, pp. 40, 42
  Rotala
    Fig. 54, p. 50

Menyanthaceae
  Menyanthes
    Fig. 105, p. 90
  Nymphoides
    Fig. 36, p. 34

Nymphaeaceae
  Brasenia
    Fig. 34, p. 33
  Cabomba
    Fig. 33, p. 32
  Nelumbo
    Fig. 35, p. 33
  Nuphar
    Fig. 37, p. 34
  Nymphaea
    Fig. 38, p. 35

Onagraceae
  (Jussiaea)
  Ludwigia
    Fig. 51, pp. 47, 48
    Fig. 83, pp. 71, 72
  Trapa
    Fig. 39, p. 36

Plantaginaceae
  Littorella
    Fig. 137, p. 119

Podostemaceae
  Podostemum
    Fig. 107, p. 91

Polygonaceae
  Polygonum
    Fig. 80, p. 69
  Rumex
    Fig. 79, p. 68

Primulaceae
  Glaux
    Fig. 25, p. 27
  Hottonia
    Fig. 115, p. 97
  Lysimachia
    Fig. 44, p. 40, 41

Ranunculaceae
  Caltha
    Fig. 70, p. 62
  Ranunculus
    Fig. 71, pp. 62, 63
    Fig. 148, p. 127

Rosaceae
  Potentilla
    Fig. 108, p. 92
    Fig. 109, p. 93

Rubiaceae
  Cephalanthus
    Fig. 29, p. 29
  Galium
    Fig. 43, p. 39

Salicaceae
  Populus *
  Salix
    Fig. 27, p. 28

Sarraceniaceae
  Darlingtonia
    Fig. 32, p. 32
  Sarracenia
    Fig. 31, p. 31

Scrophulariaceae
  Bacopa
    Fig. 50, p. 47

  Gratiola
    Fig. 60, p. 55
  Leucospora
    Fig 42, p. 39
  Limosella
    Fig. 98, p. 85
  Lindernia
    Fig. 59, p. 54
  Mimulus
    Fig. 58, p. 54
  Veronica
    Fig. 57, p. 53

Solanaceae
  Solanum
    Fig. 76, p. 66

Umbelliferae
  Angelica
    Fig. 114, p. 96
  Cicuta
    Fig. 113, p. 95
  Eryngium
    Fig. 78, p. 67
  Hydrocotyle
    Fig. 68, p. 60
  Oenanthe
    Fig. 112, p. 95
  Oxypolis
    Fig. 110, p. 94
  Sium
    Fig. 111, p. 94

Verbenaceae
  Lippia
    Fig. 64, p. 58

Violaceae
  Viola
    Fig. 97, p. 84

Index and Pictured Glossary

Figure 173

Figure 174

Figure 175

Figure 176

Fig. 177

Figure 178

Figure 179

D

Figure 180

Figure 181

Figure 182

Dermatocarpon, 12
Dianthera, 50, 51, 132
   americana, 51
   ovata, 51
DICHOTOMOUS: dividing,
   sometimes repeatedly in
   two, usually equal parts.
   Fig. 183

Figure 183

Dicotyledonae, 1
Didiplis, 131, 132
   diandra, 132
   linearis, 132
DIOECIOUS: with two sorts of
   spores, or with two sexes
   appearing on separate
   plants.
DISC FLOWER: the inner, tubular flowers of a head as in
   the Compositae.
DISSECTED: with deep divisions; deeply cut into separate parts or lobes. Fig. 184

Figure 184

Distribution, 3
DIVIDED: incisions to the
   base; deeply cut into separate parts. Fig. 185

Figure 185

Division (Phylum), 8
Dock, 68, 75
Dcgwood, 29
   Red Ozier, 29
DORSAL: referring to the back;
   the top side as opposed to
   the under or ventral surface.

DORSIVENTRAL: a thallus or
   plant part showing a dif-
   ferentiation between top
   and bottom.
Drepanocladus, 22, 23, 106
Dropwort, 93, 102, 113
Drosera, 78
   linearis, 78
   rotundifolia, 78
Droseraceae, 78
Drying Plants, 6
Duckweed, 103
   Great, 13, 24, 42, 103
   Star, 103
   Strap-shaped, 103
Dulichium, 143, 144
   arundinaceum, 144

E

Echinodorus, 83, 89
   cordifolius, 83
Ecology, 3
Economic Importance, 2
Eel Grass, 137
Eichhornia crassipes, 77
Elatinaceae, 49
Elatine, 49 51, 105
   americana, 49
   triandra, 49
Eleocharis, 115, 140
   albida, 116
   obtusa, 116
   palustris, 116
ELLIPSOID: like an ellipse;
   elliptic. Fig. 186

Figure 186

ELLIPTIC: in the shape of an
   ellipse; oval with poles narrowly rounded. Fig. 187

Figure 187

Elodea, vii, 3, 37, 45
   canadensis, 37, 38
   densa, 37
   occidentalis, 37
EMERGENT: Emersed: grow-
   ing above or extending
   above the water surface.
ENTIRE: a smooth or even
   margin. Fig. 188

Figure 188

Equisetaceae, 106
Equisetum, 106
   fluviatile, 106
   littorale, 106
   palustre, 106
   scirpoides, 106
EQUITANT: one part folded
   over another, appearing as
   if split lengthwise, as one
   leaf enclosing another in its
   margin. Fig. 189

Figure 189

Ericaceae, 26, 30
Eriocaulaceae, 126
Eriocaulon, 126, 129
   septengulare, 126
Eriophorum, 121, 140
Eryingium, 67, 70, 75
   prostratum, 67
Eryngo, 67, 70, 75
Euglenophyta, 1
Evolution, 2
EXSERTED: projecting beyond
   surrounding parts or beyond
   a sheath or envelope.

F

False Asphodel, 124
False Dragonhead, 56
False Loosestrife, 47, 52, 72,
   74
False Pimpernel, 54
Family, defined, 8
Fanwort, 32, 45, 98, 100
FASCICLED: bunched, as in a
   cluster of leaves on a stem.
   Fig. 21
Featherfoil, 96, 100
FILIFORM: like a thread, long,
   narrow, often lax. Fig. 190

Figure 190

Fissidens, 22, 106
Fissidentaceae, 22
Flag, 135
Flcating Fern, 42, 76, 84
Floating Heart, 34
Floating Moss, 23, 35, 60, 103
FLORET: a single grass flow-
   er; referring to one of a
   cluster or spike of flowers.
Flowering Quillwort, 129
Flowering Rush, 125
FOLLICLE: a simple, dry fruit
   which opens by splitting
   along an inner side. Fig. 191

Figure 191

Fontinalaceae, 22
Fontinalis, 21, 22, 106
   antipyretica, 22
Food, Animals and Man, 2
Forget-me-not, 70
Fox-tail Grass, 110
FRINGE: hairs or membrane
   along a margin. Fig. 192

Figure 192

Frogbit, 76, 83
Frog-fruit, 58
FUNNELFORM: like a funnel;
   tubular but much broader
   at one end. Fig. 193

Figure 193

G

Galium, 39, 40
   tinctorium, 40
   trifidum, 40
GAMETOPHORE: a branch or
   stalk which bear sex organs.
Gases, Carbon Dioxide and
   Oxygen, 4

GEMMAE: special buds produced in the Bryophyta consisting of a number of cell, one of which is a growing point. Fig 1b
Gentianaceae, 90
Genus, defined, 8
GLABROUS: smooth, without hairs or bristles.
Glasswort, 103
Glaux, 26, 49, 52
  maritima, 27
GLOBULAR: approximately spherical.
GLOBULE: a special branch forming a globular (spherical) body that contains the antheridial cells and sperm, as in the Characeae.
GLUME: a bract at the base of a grass spikelet. Fig. 194

Figure 194

Glyceria, 107, 109
  borealis, 107
  fluitans, 107, 109
Goatweed, 45, 49, 51, 52
Golden Club, 88
Gramineae, 107, 108, 109, 110, 111, 113
Gratiola, 55
  lutea, 55
  neglecta, 55
  virginica, 55
Ground Almond, 134
Gymnospermae, 1

H

Haloragaceae, 38, 100, 104
Harpanthaceae, 21
Hedge Hyssop, 55
Hedge Nettle, 58
Hepaticae, 1
HERBACEOUS: herblike, nonwoody; annual plants.
Heteranthera, 81, 89, 116, 139
  dubia, 81
  limosa, 81
  reniformis, 81
Hippuris, 38, 40, 135
  vulgaris, 38
Hog Fennel, 93
Horn Fern, 84
Horned Pondweed, 131
Hornwort, 101
Horsetail Fern, 106
Hottonia, 96, 97, 100
  inflata, 97
Hydrilla, vii
  verticillata, 37, 38
Hydrocotyle, 60, 69, 75, 84
  americana, 60

umbellata, 60
  verticillata, 60
Hydrolea quadrivalvis, 73
Hydrophyllaceae, 73
Hydrotrida, 47, 56
Hypericaceae, 46
Hypericum, 46, 49, 51, 52
  boreale, 46
  ellipticum, 46
  punctatum, 46
  virginicum, 46
Hypnaceae, 23

I

IMBRICATE: overlapping as in bud scales, or overlapping of leaves on a stem. Fig. 195

Figure 195

INCISED: with sharp cuts along a margin, sometimes deep. Fig. 196

Figure 196

Indian Rice, 107
INFERIOR OVARY: an ovary below other flower parts; with the perianth attached at the top of the ovary.
INTERNODE: a section of a stem axis between nodes or joints.
INVOLUCRE: scales, bracts or leaves subtending reproductive flower parts, or subtending a group of flowers.
Iridaceae, 135
Iris, 135
  fulva, 135
  pseudacorus, 135
  versicolor, 135
Isoetaceae, 126
Isoetes, 126

J

JOINT: a section or portion; a unit of a thallus. Fig 197

Figure 197

Juncaceae, 114
Juncaginaceae, 124, 129
Juncus, 114, 140
  effusus, 115
  nodosus, 115
Jungermanniales, 21
Jussiaea, 47, 71, 72, 74
  decurrens, 71
  diffusa, 71
Justicia, 51, 132

K

Kalmia, 28
  augustifolia, 28, 29
  polifolia, 28

L

Labiatae, 56, 57, 59
Labrador Tea, 28
Lake Cress, 64, 75, 99
LANCEOLATE: lance-shaped; narrowly elliptic and tapering at both ends. Fig. 198

Figure 198

Larch, 24
Larix laricina, 24, 25
Leafy Liverworts, 21
Leather Leaf, 28, 30
Ledum groenlandicum, 28, 30
Leersia, 111
LEMMA: one of the two scales about the reproductive parts of a grass flower, the other being the palea. Fig. 199. Plate I.

Figure 199

Lemna, 15, 24, 103
  minor, 15

trisulca, 103
  valdiviana, 14
Lemnaceae, 20
Lentibulariaceae, 98
Leucospora, 39, 42, 53, 101
  multifida, 39
Lichen, 39
Light Relationships, 3
LIGULE: a thin scale or membrane across the base of a leaf or at the top of the sheath in the grass family; also applied to a strapshaped corolla as in the Compositae. Fig. 200

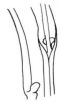

Figure 200

Lilaea subulata, 129
Liliaceae, 125
Limnobium, 76, 77, 83
  spongia, 77
Limosella, 85, 126, 128
  aquatica, 85
  subulata, 85
Lindernia, 54
  anagallidea, 54
  dubia, 54
LINEAR: a narrow and elongate shape (leaf or lobe); several times longer than broad with parallel or subparallel margins usually. Fig. 201

Figure 201

Lippia, 58
  lanceolata, 58
  nodiflora, 58
Littorella, 119, 128
  americana, 119
Liverworts, 1, 12, 15
LOBE: a part extended from the whole; a segment.
Lobelia, 69, 78
  cardinalis, 70
  dortmanna, 70
Lobeliaceae, 70
Loosestrife, 40, 50, 51, 72, 73
Lophotocarpus, 80, 81
Lotus, 33
Ludwigia, 47, 52, 72, 74
  linearis, 47
  palustris, 47
  polycarpa, 47
Luzula, 114

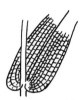

Figure 202

O

Figure 203

Figure 204

Figure 205

P

Figure 206

Figure 207

Figure 208

Figure 209

Figure 210

Phyllospadix scouleri, 136, 137
Physostegia virginiana, 56, 57
Picea mariana, 24
Pickerelweed, 82, 89
Pigmy Weed, 48, 105
PINNATE: like a feather; a compound leaf with leaflets arranged along an axis; lobings featherlike. Fig. 211

Figure 211

Pipewort, 126, 129
Pistia stratioides, 76
PISTIL: the female reproductive part of a flower including an ovary, style (usually present as a slender stalk) and a stigma (pollen receiver).
Pitcher Plant, 31
Plantaginaceae, 119
POD: a dry, many-seeded fruit such as characteristic of the pea family. See Silique.
Podostemaceae, 91
Podostemum, 91, 136
ceratophyllum, 91
Polygonaceae, 68, 69
Polygonum, 68, 69
coccineum fa. *natans*, 69
hydropiperoides, 69
natans, 69
setaceus, 69
Pondweed, 42, 52, 68, 75, 136, 139
Pontederia, 82, 89
cordata, 82
Pontederiaceae, 77, 82
Pool Moss, 105
Potamogeton, vii, 3, 4, 42, 44, 52, 68, 75, 136, 139
amplifolius, 44
crispus, 52, 53, 75
gramineus, 44
natans, 44
pectinatus, 44
praelongus, 44
richardsonii, 44
robbinsii, 44
zosteriformis, 44

Potamogetonaceae, 44, 53, 137
Potentilla, 92
anserina, 92
pacifica, 92
palustris, 93
Primulaceae, 27, 97
Proserpinaca, 67, 75, 93
palustris var. *amblyogona*, 67
Psilopsida, 1
Pteropsida, 1
PUBESCENT: with hairs, usually soft and short.
Pyrrhophyta, 1

Q

Quillwort, 126

R

RACEME: an inflorescence with stalked flowers arranged along a common axis. Fig. 212

Figure 212

Ranunculaceae, 62, 127
Ranunculus, 4, 62, 66, 74, 93, 98, 127
ambigens, 62
aquatilis, 62
flabellaris, 62
hederaceous, 74
laxicaulis, 62
purshii, 62
repens, 62
reptans, 62, 127
reptans var. *ovalis*, 62
RAY FLOWERS: the petal-like, marginal flowers of a Compositae inflorescence around the central, tubular flowers; sometimes the entire head composed of Ray Flowers as in *Chrysanthemum* cultivated, or Dandelion.
RECEPTACLE: the top of the pedicle which bears flower parts; or the top of a flowering shoot which bears many flowers; a supporter of other parts.
Red Ozier Dogwood, 29
RENIFORM: kidney-shaped; bean-shaped. Fig. 213

Figure 213

REVOLUTE: with enrolled margins.
RHIZOID: a fine hairlike extension of a cell forming an anchoring or absorbing organ.
RHIZOME: a thick, horizontal underground stem.
Rhodophyta, 1, 19
RHOMBOID: somewhat quadrangular with rounded corners.
Riccia fluitans, 15
Ricciaceae, 15
Ricciocarpus natans, 15
Riverweed, 91, 136
ROOTSTOCK: a thickened basal part of a plant with rootlike characters.
Rorippa, 35, 64, 94
aquatica, 64
nasturtium-aquaticum, 65
palustris, 64
sylvestris, 64
Rosaceae, 93
Rotala, 50, 134
diandra, 50
ramosior, 50
ROTATE: circular; disclike. Fig. 214

Figure 214

Royal Fern, 89
Rubiaceae, 30
Rumex, 68, 75
verticillatus, 68
Ruppia, 128, 136
maritima, 128
Ruppiaceae, 128
Rush, 114, 140
Rhynchospora, 145
alba, 145
macrostachya, 145

S

Sagittaria, 3, 79, 89, 119
cristata, 79
cuneata, 79
latifolia, 79
subulata, 79
SAGGITATE: arrow-shaped.
Saint John's-wort, See St. John's-wort.
Salicaceae, 28

Salicornia, 103
Salix serissima, 27, 28
SALVERFORM: a V-shaped tube with a broadened, rotate opening. Fig. 215

Figure 215

Salvinia, 23, 24, 35, 42, 60, 103
Salviniaceae, 23, 24
Sand Spury, 133
Sarracenia, 31, 32
drummondii, 31
purpurea, 31
Sarraceniaceae, 31
SCAPE: a flowering shoot (usually without leaves) arising from a basal position.
Scirpus, 113
americanus, 114, 144
atrocinctus, 114
atrovirens, 114
hudsonianus, 143
subterminalis, 122
validus, 114
Scrophulariaceae, 39, 47, 53, 54
Scutellaria, 55
epilobiifolia, 56
laterifolia, 56
Sea Blite, 138
Sea Cow, 77
Sea Milkwort, 26, 49, 52
Sedge, 134, 140, 144
SERRATE: sharply toothed along the margin. Fig. 216

Figure 216

SHEATH: a thin (usually) membranous expansion of a petiole base which encloses the stem wholly or in part; a scalelike collar which surrounds the stem at the nodes.
SHEATHING: one leaf partly enclosing another at their bases; a leaf base partly or wholly enclosing a stem.
SICKLE-SHAPED: sharply crescent-shaped.

SILIQUE: the pod fruit of the mustard family consisting of two (usually) chambers (locules), the two parts separating from a central axis at maturity. Fig. 217

Figure 217

Sium, 94, 98
  suave, 94
Skullcap, 55
Skunk Cabbage, 85
Slough Grass, 112
Smartweed, 68
Solanaceae, 66
Solanum dulcamara, 66, 69
SPADIX: a flowering shoot, usually thick bearing a compact head or cylinder of many small flowers, usually enclosed by a broad sheath, the spathe (q.v.).
Sparganiaceae, 118
Sparganium, 117, 118, 138
  androcladum, 118
  chlorocarpum, 118
  fluctuans, 118
Spartina, 112, 113
  pectinata, 113
SPATHE: a broad involucral scale or a membranous envelope about a spadix (q.v.). Fig. 218

Figure 218

SPATULATE: a figure (leaf) decidedly broader and rounded at the apex, narrowing toward the base. Fig. 219

Figure 219

Spearmint, 59
Species, defined, 8
Speedwell, 53, 55
Spergularia, 133
  canadensis, 133
Spermatophyta (Spermatopsida), 1
Sphagnaceae, 21
Sphagnum, 20, 21
  magellanicum, 21
  rubellum, 21
Sphenopsida, 1
SPIKE: a straight, stout inflorescence with flowers closely arranged along the axis at the apex of the stem or lateral shoot.
Spiked Loosestrife, 40, 49, 50, 52
Spike Rush, 115, 140
SPIKELET: a branch of a spike; a small portion of an inflorescence bearing a few (or only one) flowers; see grasses and sedges. Fig. 220

Figure 220

Spirodela, 13, 24, 42, 103
  polyrhiza, 14
SPORANGIOPHORE: a stem, branch, or a stalk which bears sporangia, the sporangiophores usually arranged to form a cone or strobilus as in *Equisetum* and the Lycopsida.
SPOROCARP: a nutlike body including several sporangia (a covered sorus) as in *Salvinia* and *Marsilea*. Fig. 221

Figure 221

Stachys, 58
  homotricha, 58
  tenuifolia, 58
Star Duckweed, 103
STIGMA: the pollen-collecting surface of a pistil.
STIPULE: a winglike or scalelike organ attached to the base of a leaf petiole or on the stem at the point of leaf attachment; the stipule sometimes taking the form of a thorn, or a tendril. Fig. 222

Figure 222

St. Johns's-wort, 46, 49, 51, 52
Stonewort, 16
Strap-shaped Duckweed, 103
Suaeda, 138
  depressa, 139
  linearis, 139
  maritima, 139
  torreyana, 139
Subularia, 119, 120, 126, 129
  aquatica, 120
SUCCULENT: thick and fleshy, swollen and often juicy.
Sundew, 78
Surf Grass, 136
Swamp Laurel, 28
Swamp Loosestrife, 36, 51
Sweet Flag, 120
Symplocarpus foetidus, 85

T

Tamarack, 25
Taxodiaceae, 25
Taxodium distichum, 25
Taxon, defined, 8
TENDRIL: a twisted or coiled, slender outgrowth of a stem or petiole by which climbing plants cling.
TERETE: round in cross section.
TERNATE: with major divisions in 3's; pinnately compound leaves with the terminal leaflets arranged in 3's. Fig. 223

Figure 223

THALLUS: a plant body without true roots, stem and leaves.
Three-way Sedge, 143
Tillaea, 48, 105
  aquatica, 49
Tofieldia, 124
  glutinosa, 125
Tolypella, 19
Tooth-cup, 50, 134
TRANSLUCENT: permitting light to pass through, not entirely transparent.
Trapa natans, 36
TRICHOMATOUS: having hairs.
TRICHOTOMUS: divided or forked into 3 equal (usually) parts.
TRIFURCATE: forking into 3 parts.
Triglochin, 123, 124, 129
  maritima, 124
Trumpets, 31
TRUNCATE: flattened at the apex; abruptly rounded at the apex. Fig. 224

Figure 224

TUBERCLE: a thickened (often pointed) knob at the apex of a nutlet. Fig. 225

Figure 225

TUBULAR: a hollow structure with parallel margins; a long, slender corolla.
TUBULAR FLOWER: the central flowers in the inflorescence of the Compositae, shaped in the form of a tube. Fig. 226

Figure 226

Twig Rush, 144
Typha, 138
  angustifolia, 138
  latifolia, 138
Typhaceae, 138

U

UMBEL: a flat-topped inflorescence, either simple or compound (with several smaller umbels involved to form an inflorescence). Fig. 227.

Figure 227

Umbelliferae, 60, 94, 95, 96
UNDULATE: with a wavy margin, or with a wavy surface. Fig. 228

Figure 228

Use of Key, 9
UTRICLE: a membranous bladderlike covering of a fruit or seeds.
Utricularia, 31, 97, 98, 102, 104, 107
  cornuta, 98
  intermedia, 98
  minor, 98
  purpurea, 98, 102
  vulgaris, 98

V

Vaccinium, 25, 26, 30
  macrocarpon, 26
  oxycoccus, 26
Vallisneria, 117
  americana, 117
  neotropicalis, 117
VALVE: a chamber or section of a compound ovary; a locule.
VENTRAL: the lower or under side.
Verbena, 58
Verbenaceae, 58
Veronica, 53, 55
  americana, 53
VERTICIL: a whorl of flower-bearing stalks at a stem node or stem tip. Fig. 229

Figure 229

Viola lanceolata, 84
Violaceae, 84
Violet, 84

W

Water Arum, 61, 69, 82
Water Celery, 95, 117
Water Chestnut, 36
Water Cress, 65, 69, 93
Water Fern, 20, 23, 35, 60, 103
Water Hemlock, 95, 100
Water Hemp, 74
Water Horehound, 59
Water Hyacinth, 77
Water Hyssop, 47, 52, 54, 56
Water Lettuce, 76
Water Lily, 35, 61
Water Mare's Tail, 38, 40, 135
Water Marigold, 57, 100
Water Meal, 14
Water Parsnip, 94, 98
Water Pennywort, 60, 69, 75, 84
Water Plantain, 87
Water Primrose, 72, 74
Water Purslane, 131
Water Shield, 33
Water Spearwort, 127
Water Starwort, 45, 131
Water Velvet, 103
Water Weed, 37, 45

Water Willow, 26, 50, 132
Waterwort, 49, 51, 105
WHORLED: with several leaves, scales or branches arising at one level from all sides of a stem or axis.
Widgeon Grass, 128, 136
Wild Rice, 107
Willow, 27
Wolffia, 14
  columbiana, 15
  papulifera, 15
  punctata, 15
Wolffiella, 14, 103
  floridana, 14

X

Xyridaceae, 123
Xyris, 122, 123
  torta, 123

Y

Yellow-eyed Grass, 122
Yellow Skunk Cabbage, 86
Yellow Water Lily, 61

Z

Zanichellia, 131
  palustris, 131
Zanichelliaceae, 131
Zizania, 107
  aquatica, 107
  texana, 107
Zonation, 4
Zostera, 137
  marina, 137
ZYGOMORPHIC: irregular, as a corolla with unequal petals, or differently shaped petals, often a bilobed corolla.

NOTES

NOTES